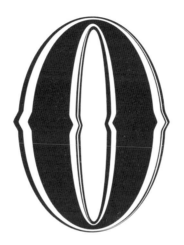

D1484682

POCKET BOOKS
New York London Toronto Sydney

PHOTO CONTRIBUTORS:

Leslie Burrell

Trent Grandberry

Chris Stokes

Randy Butler: 52, 55, 61, 63, 69, 71, 72, 78, 81, 86, 88, 90, 91, 93, 110

Kimo Easterwood: ii, xiv, 12, 32, 50, 66, 82, 94, 108

An Original Publication of MTV Books/Pocket Books

books   POCKET BOOKS

POCKET BOOKS, a division of Simon & Schuster, Inc.
1230 Avenue of the Americas, New York, NY 10020

ISBN: 1-4165-0328-5

First MTV Books/Pocket Books trade paperback edition February 2005

10 9 8 7 6 5 4 3 2

Design by thebrm
Cover credit: Kimo Easterwood

For information regarding special discounts for bulk purchases,
please contact Simon & Schuster Special Sales at 1-800-456-6798
or business@simonandschuster.com

Dedication

TO MY FAMILY AND ALL OF MY FANS WHO HAVE BEEN THERE FOR ME SINCE DAY ONE

Acknowledgments

These are for the countless people in my life that I have been guided by, and even without them knowing, their experiences have helped me to become the person I am today. Therefore, without further ado, these are my acknowledgments: To my moms, I love you! To my family, nana, auntie, and all the rest of the gang, I love you. Also, much love to pops and the rest of the family. In addition, Chris Stokes who had a great deal to do with me coming into my manhood. As well as Marques "MH" Houston, Jerome "Young Rome" Jones, Kelton "LDB" Kessee, Tony Scott, and to Miss Ketrina "Taz" Askew, my other mother, I love you, too! The boys DeMario, Jarell, and Dreux—much love, fellas; I hope all is well with you and yours. To my wonderful fans who have held me down, I love you all. Last but not least, God, you are number one in my life. Thank you for placing the people in my life to help shape and mold the spiritual man that I have become, to serve you fully is my ultimate goal in life. I love you, thanks to everyone, my high school buddies, and my homies back in the wood. Much love to everyone. Peace.

Omari Grandberry

I EXPECTED THE CALL to come through even up to the last minute, but the hours were ticking down to the show and the phone still hadn't rung.

I'm not going to lie to you—I was starting to get a little nervous. Here I was, alone in a hotel room high over downtown Philadelphia with the show three hours away, and I'm waiting for the phone to ring. I had one phone in my hand and one in my pocket, 'cuz when the call finally came I wasn't going to miss it. Every now and then I found myself just staring at the phone in my hand, like I was trying to will it to ring. A mind-over-matter thing. It wasn't working. I killed some time by staring out of the window at the cold, gray Philly sky. There were still traces of grimy snow on the ground, and the scene matched my mood. Suddenly both lines rang at once, and I was jolted from my thoughts. I flipped open a phone in each hand. My manager, Chris Stokes, was on one line. The limo driver was on the other. Neither call was what I was looking for. The driver said he was ready to run me over to the arena whenever I was, and Chris and Taz were ready to meet me there. I couldn't wait any longer, so I grabbed my gear and split.

As I watched the dreary scenery zip past, I started to wonder how things could have got so screwed up so fast. Just a few weeks ago my group, B2K, was on top of the world. I mean, we were BIG TIME. Our albums always went gold and platinum. No effort. The singles would hit the top ten easily. The videos that we were making were guaranteed heavy rotation on BET and MTV. Our live tour was selling out in

every city we went to. We were on the covers of practically every teen music and fan magazine out there. Our first movie, *You Got Served,* was in the can, completed and approaching a release date. We were running the trailer to the movie on big screens at our concerts. Two times at each show. The audiences were really into it, and I knew we had another sensation on our hands. B2K was rolling, and it felt good—and the best part was that the four of us were tight. They were my brothers, and I knew they had my back just like I had theirs.

So why am I sitting by myself in a limo, on the way to a sold-out arena in Philadelphia, wondering if my best friends, Raz-B, Lil' Fizz and J-Boog, will show up for the concert? I don't know what they're planning to do, 'cuz except for one brief conference call a few days back, we aren't talking to each other—my boys and I are communicating mostly by managers and magazine articles— when just a few weeks ago we were shooting hoops and playing Xbox.

That's what the phone call was all about. Will my boys be there to perform with me or not?

Our tour was winding up when shit started to go down. As soon as the newspapers and fan magazines realized something was up, they jumped on us. Stories were flying that we hated each other—I even heard one rumor that Raz-B, Lil' Fizz and J-Boog had told their manager they didn't want to fly on the same plane as me.

In the middle of all of this madness we still had two live shows left on the tour schedule—

Philadelphia and New York, two of our biggest fan bases. I wasn't going to let down our fans, and in my heart I felt like the boys would do what was right and show up.

We had already spent too much time being mad at each other. Way too much time, in my opinion. I had spent the last three weeks being mad at everybody and everything. I was mad at anybody else who let this dispute get very out of hand. Now it was time to put all of that stuff aside. We had some more shows to do.

Philly and New York were out there waiting for us, true fans who had bought tickets. The way I was playing it was that we still had a bond and a responsibility to our fans. We had said that B2K was going to do these shows, simple as that. Of course, things were so crazy that the other guys had lawyers telling them not to show up, but I couldn't get with that. No matter what the beefs were, I felt it was our duty to deliver. Beyond what the lawyers and managers and agents were saying, we had a responsibility to our fans—they had bought the tickets 'cuz they loved us, *all* of us, and for all of us not to show up was just disrespectful to them. The right thing to do was to finish out the tour dates we had signed up for and then, when all of that was wrapped up, get back into all of the legal and personal hassles.

As the limo sped through the Philly streets, I heard one of the local radio DJs send a shout out to "all of you on your way to see B2K!" We had to do this. I knew that the other guys in B2K felt the same way. The bottom line was that we had a bond. We were going through some stuff, but these were still my friends. Always will be. I'd talked to them about it a few days before the scheduled Philly show. I knew these guys, we'd ridden hard together for a long time. As we'd talked over the static of a four-way conference call, I had felt how torn they'd been. After all, we all wanted the same thing, to play for our fans. When I'd hung up the phone with them, I'd felt good. They weren't going to leave me hanging, they'd show up for Philly.

Don't misunderstand, I've got confidence in my singing and my ability to give it up for an audience. But this new development, the possible solo thing, had come up all of a sudden, and to be honest, it was kind of scary and intimidating. But I had committed to go on with the show with or without the other guys, and I was locked in. As the limo sped closer to the arena, I tried to prepare myself mentally, running through the new dance moves and coming up with ways to keep the show as on point as it would be with all four of us.

I concentrated on my thoughts, and some of the bs faded away. No matter how many people were on stage tonight, I knew I could find the art in what I do, and that a great performance would flow out if I could stop the doubts that were creeping into my heart.

It all came down to one question: If I had to, could I deliver what the fans were expecting? I guess doubts are a natural thing, but, man, I was not liking the way I was feeling.

One of my phones rang in the limo. It was my mom. She wished me good luck and told me to be strong. I told her I would call her after the show. I can depend on my mom to always be there with support and encouragement. Always.

Coming up on the arena, we drove past a group of fans lining up outside. Several of the younger ones were accompanied by their parents. But most of them were carrying B2K signs, wearing our T-shirts and caps and holding on to our CDs. As we pulled into the back, I checked out the building from the outside. B2K played this spot before, and I remember that we turned it out; I knew we had

some serious fans here. But going in this time was different—the last time we were four going in. This time it was only one person entering, and all of a sudden this building was looking real huge—like a fortress or something.

Now it was less than two hours before showtime. As I was going about prepping for the show, I saw constant reminders of who was not there. There was no way to get away from it. The main dressing room area was laid out for four people, but I was the only one there. I stowed my gear and went out into the arena for a mic check.

Four cordless mics were set up on stage, and I checked all four just to make sure. Behind me there were two dancers—Sam and Dave—rehearsing. These guys had been brought in to back me up if it came to me going on alone. They had good moves, but some immediate adjustments had to be made on my part if we were going to perform together that night. I'm used to glancing to my left or my right and seeing Raz or Fizz or Boog working it beside me. We were so tight I always felt that I could sense what was happening on the stage at every moment during our show. This new setup was going to be kind of strange. Sam and Dave could back me up with the choreography, but the singing was going to be all me.

I moved out into the empty arena. I took a seat halfway back and checked out the surroundings. This was something that me and the guys did before most shows. We would go out into the empty arena and hang for a few minutes—just us. It was part of our ritual. It would relax us and help get us focused. We would goof, talk trash, get ready and laugh a lot. It was like we were sizing up the battlefield where B2K was set to take on the world. We took on the world, and we always won.

Now, sitting out there alone in the arena, I felt isolated. A couple of weeks ago I was a member of a team—an elite, precision team and the hottest act out there. And now it was coming down to me facing that same B2K audience alone. That was a lot to live up to and a whole lot to prove. It was starting to feel like Omarion against the entire universe.

Back when we were working our shows, there would be several times during each performance when I'd be alone on the stage. Usually on a ballad like "Gots Ta Be." You know the setup: blue spotlights, seductive mood, nice and intimate. Our shows were tightly choreographed, and we were good at it. When I was out there by myself, I knew it was only a matter of time before the others would be right there with me smashing it. This was way different. I didn't know what to expect.

My mind went back to the last show we did together. Even though things had gotten a little tense between us by that time, we'd tossed all that aside because we were going on in five. Before hitting the stage, we'd done the thing we did before each show. The prayers and the hugs had felt different. More solemn, almost. Maybe we'd all felt the same thing that night; whatever it had been, everybody had been serious, and we'd given a killer show.

Now I'm sitting about twenty rows back from the stage, checking everything out. In an hour this place was going to fill up with excited young people. They were coming with their energy and their own expectations. As I sat and thought about what I was going to do, my cell rang. Damn, waiting on this call was getting to be a bad joke. I flipped open the phone and listened to a solid minute of loud static. I could hear what sounded like a voice, trying to communicate with me, but it was too broken up. I'll never know who made that call, but some part of me hoped it was one of the guys, calling to explain things or just to talk. Something about that failed call helped my mind to focus. I had work to do. I got up out of the seat and headed toward the back.

The crew for the night's opening act, ATL, had arrived and was hanging out backstage. I worked out a few last-minute moves with Sam and Dave and then went into the dressing room. I needed to get my head together for what was coming.

I sat alone in the room and tried to concentrate. Behind me I could feel ATL's bass line vibrating through the walls. The countdown was on. I sat back and tried to concentrate on what was immediately ahead of me, and as I closed my eyes, I had a brief daydream, one where the guys show up, charge in and make the last-minute save. Just like the cavalry. I imagined them running into the arena just as I'm about to take the stage. We grab hands, say our prayer, and then the lights come up on us. The crowd goes wild. I knew it was a fantasy, but I wanted to believe in it. I took comfort in it. But I guess if I had been listening instead of wishing, I would have known that the fantasy was bogus. As the minutes ticked by, it was becoming obvious that it was not going to happen. That didn't stop me from hoping, though.

A knock on the door. My managers, Chris and Taz, came in, and the fantasy ended. I opened my eyes and looked in the mirror. I was dressed in my Lakers jersey, and I looked good. The three other jerseys, one each for Raz-B, Lil' Fizz and J-Boog, were still hanging at the back of the room.

Chris cracked open a Coke, and we just sat there and chilled for a minute. I appreciated him being there. Taz stuck her head in and flashed five fingers at us—five minutes to showtime. This was it, no turning back, no more wishing. I finally took the phone out of my hand and tossed it into my bag. If I was going to make it or break it as a solo performer, now was the time. This was new territory that I was stepping into. If I sucked, the world was going to know it soon enough: with text messaging and the Internet, word gets around fast.

Chris told me simply to do my best, and that was it. Everything else had already been said. I left the dressing room. Outside the dancers were heading toward the stage; one of them gave me a thumbs-up. I nodded, but I've got to tell you, I still wasn't feeling it. I started moving toward the stage. As I got closer I could hear the chant building—"B2K! B2K! B2K!" It felt like I was marching up to a firing squad, and there was nothing sweet about it. But this wasn't a firing squad. They were fans; they knew me, and they knew what they wanted from me. It was my job now to deliver.

Finally I was backstage. The stage was dark, and I could feel the audience's energy building. I closed my eyes and tried to take myself into the zone. Too much stuff was running through my head, though. The lights flashed up, and just before I ran on I took one last look behind me. I knew my three bandmates wouldn't be there, but I looked anyhow. I took a deep breath and hit the stage.

Looking back, there's not too much that I remember about that performance. It was like I was outside of myself, and looking in, scrutinizing every dance step and every note. It was a trip. I gave a solid performance—the beats were as hot as always, the romantic songs as fly as ever—but I knew it just wasn't what the audience was expecting. I wanted to explain to the fans what had happened, wanted to share the emotions in my own heart, but it never happened, things were moving too fast. What I remember clearly was the chant starting up halfway through my set. "B2K! B2K! B2K!" It just got louder and louder. I tried to look out into the crowd and see their faces, because I honestly didn't know if they were chanting for me or against me at the same time. It felt like I was trying to step into my future, but I was being overwhelmed by my past. That was brutal.

Everything else after the concert was kind of a blur as well. The backstage area that night was quiet. Usually, after coming off of a good performance, the energy is high, and a lot of people are buzzing around. They are trying to be with you, networking, offering up congratulations and just wanting to hang out. That night was different. I can't remember who came back to the dressing room, but I know it wasn't too many people. Which was good, because I really wasn't into the backstage thing that night. I called my mother and told her everything had gone OK. I could tell by her voice that she didn't believe me.

After we left the arena we went back to the hotel, and I went right up to my room. We weren't going to leave for New York until the next day, and that was fine with me. I didn't want to be bothered. A couple of our road people suggested that we hang out and maybe get something to eat, but I could tell they felt bad for me and wanted to ease me through the rough reception that I'd just gotten. I declined the invitation. I just wanted to be by myself so I could go over what had just happened. I knew that there would be suggestions, advice and coaching, but all of that could wait. I just needed to get by myself and figure this thing out. I don't like being cooped up in hotel rooms, but that night it was where I needed to be—alone.

Reality hit me hard. The guys were gone, and they weren't coming back. That was all there was to it, and I wasn't even going to trip on it anymore. At some point there might be a reunion. But not now. Suddenly I was a solo performer, and that's what I had to concentrate on. If I was going to survive and thrive in this game and become the all-around entertainer that I wanted to be, I had to work it out for myself. I decided then that nobody could define me, or who I am, but me. And that's what I set out to do—define me. If anyone was going to fix this thing—being rejected by my fans—it was going to have to be me.

It rained for the rest of the evening. That fit; it had been that kind of a night. I stepped out onto my balcony high over Philadelphia. The rain was coming down hard, and it felt like sharp, freezing needles on my skin. I turned my face up and let the rain pound away. Somehow it felt good. I looked over the city and promised that I would be back. This wasn't over.

I woke up feeling different, better somehow. I'd faced the worst situation I could have imagined—going onstage without the guys—and survived. It hadn't been an easy show, but I had proved to myself that I could get it done solo.

During the ride up to New York I didn't get a single call. That was fine, I wasn't expecting any. I knew now that I was on my own, and instead of being afraid, I was excited by the challenge. If Philly had been tough, New York would be even tougher, but I felt like a soldier going into battle, and I knew I was going to win.

At the venue, I didn't go out into the audience before showtime, like I always did. I was going to change up the pattern. I needed the strength and courage of four men tonight, so I stayed in my dressing room alone. No visitors or well-wishers allowed.

Showtime. Right before I went out to the stage, one of the dancers looked at me and said, "You got it tonight, man." Maybe he saw it in my eyes, because I didn't hang back like I did in Philly. I almost sprinted to the stage, I was charging them. I knew I would take no prisoners tonight.

We broke into the first number, and I could feel the uncertainty in the audience. They wanted to be convinced, but they just didn't know what to expect. I knew they needed me to prove to them that I was still worthy of their love. We were sliding into the third number when I heard the chant begin. Near the front of the stage, a few girls began to cry out, "B2K! B2K! B2K!" I could see other girls a few rows away starting to pick up

on it. Man, why now? I could feel it from the stage. Each "B2K!" hit me like an arrow, and I knew that those little wounds could add up to some big-time pain. I was just starting to connect with the crowd and feel the energy flow back and forth between us. The chant wasn't going to do anything except break up my concentration and screw up the show.

So I charged them. I went downstage, as close as I could get without climbing off. I focused in on them like a laser. I put the song on them. I made eye contact and let them know that I was for real. It was like I was performing for each of them personally. I gave it up—and so did they. They abandoned the chant and got into what I was seriously laying on them. The rest of the audience saw what I was doing and roared in approval. They loved it, and they let me know. I was in the zone. I was trying to kill it. You know what? I was killing it. When I left the stage it was through cheers, shouts and a standing O. I know every moment can't be perfect—but this was close.

Backstage after the show was completely different in New York. The congratulations were coming in, and I loved it. I knew then that I could do this. I could get up on stage and make this happen. Whatever I put my mind to, I could accomplish. A burden had been lifted off of me like you wouldn't believe.

I learned a lot about myself and the world in that couple of days. After the New York show, I felt like I could do anything. But I also found out that if you want to be a superstar, you've got to hang and take the good with the bad. I'm hanging, and I intend to keep hanging. In my mind, what it all comes down to is keeping your focus, making mistakes and learning. Most definitely.

New York was my first successful outing as a solo performer and an all-around entertainer. It was most definitely a major turning point for me.

Chapter I

EARLY TIMES

THEY ALWAYS TOLD ME THAT I DIDN'T CRY…

WHEN I WAS BORN, I was not like any normal kid that comes crying out of the womb; I didn't make a sound. My grandmother delivered me at home, and after they wiped all of the stuff off, I just looked around the room at everybody. It was like I was saying, "I'm here." My grandmother and my aunts were all there, a room full of witnesses. They all say I didn't cry. All newborn babies cry; for some reason, I didn't. Nobody could figure it out. They were worried, and for a minute they thought that something was wrong with me. My mom, Leslie, saw it this way: She says I was announcing to the world that I had arrived, and not crying was my way of showing the universe, early on, that I was going to be different. I like her explanation, and I'll stick with that one—it's as good as any. That date was November 12, 1984, at about midnight. I'm a true Scorpio.

When I sit back and think about stuff like that—me coming into the world without shedding a tear—it makes me think, *Dang, maybe I am special, maybe I'm here for a reason.*

Me and my mother have been tight from the beginning. Leslie Burrell was only sixteen when she had me. For a while, there was a little pressure on

her to give me up for adoption at birth or have an abortion so she could continue going to school. She insisted that there was a special bond formed when I was growing inside of her and that she wanted to keep me. Soon the rest of the family got on board, and everybody was very supportive.

I'm glad that things turned out the way they did. I couldn't have been raised in a more loving and supportive household. We lived in a two-story house on Bronson Avenue in Los Angeles. The neighborhood was middle-class working people. I remember it being a fairly safe place at the time. But the thing I remember most was that the house on Bronson was overflowing with love.

My mother was in high school when she had me. She would go to school and place a picture of me on her desk. My Nana—that's my grandmother—raised me. My mother would rush home from school to see her son. She would tell me that on days I would fall asleep before she got home, she would wake me up to be with me. Mom told me that she and her aunts would argue over who would babysit. When I was born, it brought a lot of joy to the house, because a baby was such new

energy. I am the first of four on my mother's side, and the first of three on my father's side. So, I'm really the first of seven.

My father wasn't in my life much when I was growing up. He was just a kid too when my mom got pregnant. He was fifteen. Soon after I was born, he got into some trouble and spent some time in prison. We have a great relationship now. He was sad, though, that he wasn't able to be there for the early, important things in my life like first steps, birthdays, holidays. I really didn't figure out that I was missing a male presence in in my life until later on. The women in my household—my mom, grandmother and aunts—gave me a lot of love, so I never really felt abandoned, or resentful or anything like that. Nobody ever talked bad about him either. When I'd ask about my father—like, where was he?—they would just say that he was away and that one day he'd be back. When we did hook up, we got along like almost immediately. He told me that it was a blessing that he hadn't been around, because I have all his good qualities but none of his bad qualities. I love my pops. Trent Grandberry is a cool dude.

I remember a lot of things growing up on Bronson—a lot of good things. When you're a kid, you never really realize how animated you are. I look at the pictures of my younger brothers and me, and it's obvious we were full of life. And when I look at my little cousins, they dance, they sing, they're so full of energy. My aunt Toni, my Nana's sister, told me I was ten times worse!

We were actually a really, really close family. There was my Nana and my great-grandmother, Nanee. I never really got to know her that well, but I remember all the hats she used to wear when she went to church. It was my great-grandmother, Nanee, that dragged me to church most Sundays. I wasn't much interested, but I sure loved to hear the choir sing. She would nudge me and say, "Sing, Omari. Sing real loud. Let the angels hear you sing." And I would.

My Nana was real old school. She would wake up real early almost every day, put on garden gloves and fix up her garden. She loved her garden—the pretty flowers, fruits, vegetables. It was real nice; I loved it out there. That whole backyard seemed spacius to me. There were grass, trees,

3

hedges, everything a kid could ask for. I spent a lot of time back there.

There was a strawberry plant in our backyard, just next to Nana's garden. Every year I would ask my Nana if I could eat some of the berries. And she would always tell me, "No, you have to wait until its time." Every day I used to go out in that yard just to see if the plant had grown a little. I guess this was my first lesson in patience. When I finally got to those strawberries, it was worth it. I haven't tasted anything as sweet since.

My best friend was our dog, Dusty. He was a German shepherd, and I used to love him. I remember when he would crawl under the house and I would go under there with him. Down there it was like I was in Dusty's world. That was our secret hangout; we stayed there for hours at a time. When he would be outside we chained him to a pole in the middle of the yard. I'd play with him and he would run around me. Before I knew it, I was wrapped up in the chain, and I would have to call Nana to untie me. "Nana, help! Come get me!" One day, when I went under the house, something strange happened—Dusty snapped at me! He bared his teeth and everything. Not long after, he died. I was going to school one morning, and my Nana told me. I was so upset, I just cried and cried. To this day I think Dusty was poisoned by one of our neighbors, who was always complaining that he barked too much. The barking didn't bother me, 'cuz that's what dogs are supposed to do. I really missed Dusty. I didn't understand how a person could feel it was all right to kill a creature that was just doing what came natural to it.

My other friend was my little brother O'Ryan. We'd spend hours in the garden practicing back flips like we'd seen people do on the television. When Nana wasn't looking, we dragged an old mattress out into the yard and just started tumbling one day. At first we weren't so good. A lot of the stuff we tried didn't work, and we missed the mattress entirely a few times, but when you're a kid you seem to bounce back quickly. When Nana realized what we were doing, she wasn't happy—she'd look up from her cooking in the kitchen and watch us from the window. Every time we did a flip she'd yell out "Omari Grandberry, you be careful! You're going to break your neck and your brother's too." She would always call me by both names when she was warning me about something or when I was in trouble. We kept at it, though, and then, later, when she looked out, we had a flying, tumbling routine that ended with me doing a back flip. Despite being annoyed at us, she had to admit we looked pretty good, and from her spot at the kitchen sink she applauded us. We even took a bow.

The same back flips that O'Ryan and I learned in the backyard are the ones that I eventually incorporated into the B2K shows.

My first school was Highland Elementary School in Inglewood, and I loved it. It was all good to me, and going to school each day, with all the different teachers and different classes, felt like an adventure.

My best memory from kindergarten was my very first girlfriend, Aja. Aja Allen had long pretty hair and big, bright eyes. We were inseparable. We used to hold hands in the cafeteria line or on the bus. With Aja as my girl "forever," I actually enjoyed going to school.

Another thing that I liked about school was the teachers. Some of mine were great. I remember my favorite—her name was Ms. Godfrey, my third-grade teacher. I just loved her. She was a hottie. All of the little boys were in love with her. She taught in an entertaining way that would keep you interested. I always thought it was cool how she could make you actually enjoy a history class, or help you learn about something that you had never been into before. She made you feel like it was cool to work. In a way, Ms. Godfrey taught me a little about being an entertainer and knowing how to connect with an audience to make people feel what you are feeling.

My other favorite teacher was Mr. Shaw. He reminded me of a wise old owl. Mr. Shaw would always lose his glasses, only to find them pushed up on the top of his head. He would come up with different songs to help us remember the names of the fifty states and things like that. Sometimes he would have us get out of our chairs and sit Indian style on the floor while he taught a particular lesson. He wasn't afraid to be different and teach in a way that the other teachers hadn't thought of. All kids should have teachers that good.

Looking back, I feel so lucky to have gone to such a positive, encouraging school. People seemed to smile and laugh a lot. Most of the students there were into it like I was, and I think a lot of us took away the feeling that the world was a good place and anything was possible. Whenever I would get into trouble, it would be for something real light, like running through the halls when I should have been walking. "Slow down, Omari. Slow down." I did—most of the time.

By the time I got to the fifth grade, they made a change in the rules so that the fifth grade, the one I was entering, would be the last grade in elementary school. Aja's family had moved away by then, so she'd transferred out to another school. I guess "forever" didn't last past the first grade.

I've always liked having a crew. Even in elementary school I had my guys—there were four of us that really hung tough in that last year of elementary school. It was me, Boner and Lovell, a.k.a. Chilli. I mean, we were tight. Boner came from a large Mexican family. Lovell was my boy. This guy was always getting into fights and always winning. He had some hands on him. Lovell was ready for action whenever and wherever. We all ended up taking boxing lessons, but Lovell was the guy with the hands. Michael Magee, we called him Big Mike, was another buddy. Throughout elementary school the two of us were always fighting each other, but we still remained pals. We spent most of our time playing basketball, but we would always manage to find ourselves in some unusual situations, sometimes bordering on getting in trouble. We weren't bad kids. We just did what boys did in the fifth grade—be boys. It's always good to have a crew—even in elementary school.

Boner and me joined up with a basketball little league out of the Rosemont Center in Inglewood. I played point guard for the Chicago Bulls team. Our uniforms were just like the real Bulls uniforms. We liked playing, but the truth is that we weren't any good. We couldn't dribble. We couldn't pass, catch or shoot. We would run down the court and throw the ball up in the stands. We'd shoot and miss the backboard altogether.

One kid would just stand in the middle of the court and watch the game go on around him. We were kind of whack—but we did our thing. We got out there and played week after week. Most of the time we lost. Boner's team waxed us every time we played together. Whatever we tried, we could never beat those guys. Every so often we would play a team that was even worse than ours, which would amaze me—how could you be worse than the worst? Our team got better, though, and by the next season we had improved quite a bit.

In the fifth grade I hooked up with my first real girlfriend, Delisa, the most beautiful girl in the school. We used to hold hands and sometimes nap side by side in class during free time. One day she passed me a note that said, "O, meet me by the girl's room." A few minutes after, she asked to be excused. I asked too, and the teacher let me go. I got my first kiss that day. I just knew I was in love. I just knew that Delisa and I were together forever. Again "forever." We actually are still in contact today. The last year in elementary school was a wonderful year. And then I was headed off to junior high.

I went to Audubon Junior High School. It was a rough school in a rough part of the hood. For my first few months there, I got teased because I wasn't from the neighborhood where most of the kids were from. At first I reacted to the teasing, and I even got in a few fights with some kids, but then I wised up and learned to ignore it. I figured I had better things to do, and besides, I didn't hate school the way those kids did. Eventually the other kids got tired of trying to get a rise out of me, and they moved on to someone else.

After a while I just kind of fit in.

Audubon is where fashion came to life in a big way. It was an incredible atmosphere for profiling. No matter what, you had to have the fly sneakers. On the day when a new pair of Air Jordans came out, the seventh and eighth graders had them on first period. Brand-new out of the box, and they made sure that everybody saw them. Those shoes

stirred up some serious trouble, and I honestly think that Air Jordans were responsible for more fights than anything else at the school. You would think that the fights would be started by someone trying to steal the shoes off of another kid, but the fights were usually between girls claiming to be the girlfriend of whoever had the newest pair of Air Jordans. Things could get really out of control—I remember one afternoon when a whole gang of girls were just screaming at each other while the boys kicked back and watched, laughing.

Sorting that stuff out—who was who, who said what—was always pretty confusing, but now that I look back on it, it was kind of like preparation for dealing with female fans later on. When B2K first hit, I couldn't believe the things girls would do to get by security and meet us. The first time a girl managed to run backstage, screaming, a three-hundred-pound bodyguard puffing after her, I thought, "Damn, just like high school!"

One thing I was always aware of was that some people like you for the things you have, or the things you can do for them, rather than who you are. One day, my boy Big Mike and I walked into the cafeteria during the fourth period. He had on a brand-new pair of Air Jordans. Girls immediately surrounded him. "Oooh, let me see." "Where'd you get them?" "How much do they cost?" This chump winked at me like he was saying, "What a player I

am." I said, "It ain't you. It's the shoes, fool!" He didn't hear. He was enjoying his little moment.

In junior high, we had different teachers for each subject. I don't remember the actual learning to be as much fun or even as interesting as it had been in elementary school. I guess it had something to do with the teachers being preoccupied with trying to keep order. The teaching suffered. I do remember a couple of teachers that actually seemed to care. One of them was Mr. Geralt. I heard that he had served in Vietnam, because a lot of the stuff that came out of his mouth sounded straight-up military. Especially when he was on hall duty. He had this megaphone, and he'd yell over it to keep order in the halls. "Young man, let's get those pants pulled up." "I suggest that you get to class on the double!" "Stand up straight! Don't slouch!" "What was that? That sounds like two hours detention." "Go! Go! Now!" He was funny. But it worked. We did what he said.

Mr. Geralt singled out some students that he thought had some potential, and I was one of them. He thought that boxing would be good for me, and he suggested I try it out. I decided to take him up on it and got involved with the boxing program at the local rec center. The boxing coach was Mr. Johnson. He was a big, old guy who really knew his stuff. He always had a cigar clenched in his teeth, but he never lit it till the end of the day. When

ALL NEWBORN BABIES CRY;
FOR SOME REASON, I DIDN'T. NOBODY
COULD FIGURE IT OUT. THEY WERE WORRIED,
AND FOR A MINUTE THEY THOUGHT
THAT SOMETHING WAS WRONG WITH ME.

you could get him talking, he would tell you the most amazing stories about the old-time boxers. It was like he knew every great boxer who ever lived.

The first thing he ever had me do was run backwards around the ring. I guess he was checking out how I could move. Then he had me punch the heavy bag for a few minutes. That was it.

After that first lesson I thought that I was it. I knew I had mad skills and wanted to show them off, and I told Coach Johnson that I couldn't wait for my first match. I got my wish a few days later when Coach Johnson put me in the ring with a kid that had been around for a while. When we stepped into the ring, Coach Johnson just kicked back with a little smile on his face. I guess he was throwing me into the deep end to see if I would sink or swim. My opponent was the younger brother of a friend of mine, and he was smaller than me, but I knew he could box a little bit. Still, I figured taking him would be no problem. I could almost feel how good victory was going to be.

The bell rang, and we squared off and went at it. I barely had my gloves up when the kid hit me with a left hook. I stumbled backwards, arms swinging wildly like a windmill. I had no stamina. No breath control. After a minute my arms were burning from the effort of holding them up. My nose was running. I was a mess. The kid landed a couple of good ones on my ribs, and I actually saw stars. I must have done something right, 'cuz at the end of the three rounds the referee called it for me, but I felt like I had lost. I promised myself then that I was going to get serious about the boxing thing. That match taught me a good lesson: Winning doesn't feel like winning when you can't be sure in your heart that you really are the best.

Coach Johnson was a good man, and in the time I trained with him my boxing skills got pretty sharp. The thing with Coach was that he knew a lot about life as well as boxing. After our workouts we would sit and talk about things that related to life beyond boxing. I didn't have a real father figure at home, and it was cool to just sit and talk about what it meant to be a man and things like that. Coach Johnson really believed that there was more to life than just the obvious things. He told me that there should be some kind of purpose in life "beyond our own individual hopes, dreams, wants and desires." It was really important to him to show us how growing into manhood is about more than competition and sexual conquest. If we lost a match, or if a girl we liked rejected us, we shouldn't feel too bad about ourselves—there would always be another match and another girl.

Our lives should stand for something; and as far as boxing was concerned, he told us that it wasn't

about beating the other guy—even though that's the whole point of the sport—it was about competing with yourself. One day he stood me in front of a mirror and said, "Omari, look into the eyes of the only person that can ever defeat you. Study him. Know him." I'm standing there staring at myself in the mirror and going, "Whoa! Now that was heavy." I've got to admit that some of that stuff I couldn't grasp at the time. But now, years later, I'm just beginning to understand what he was talking about. In the eighth grade, not long after school started, the word went around that a new, pretty girl had transferred in. If she was as fly as the rumors had it, I wanted to meet her, and I hustled to the classroom extra quick so I could be the first to say hello. We looked at each other and smiled. There was something about her that I recognized.

She said, "You look familiar."

"Aja?"

"Omari, it is you!"

We got back together immediately, and this time we were really kicking it. We were older now, and I felt like a real man with a girl as beautiful as Aja to go around with. I felt like fate had come along and put us back together. She was my "forever" girl, again. We were doing fine, and I thought I was in love, until one of my boys told me that somebody else had been kissing my girl. I went, "What?!?"

I confronted her later that day during a fire drill. She admitted it but said it wasn't a big thing. I was still her boyfriend. I couldn't believe her—what does it mean to be a girlfriend and boyfriend if you're not going to be there for each other, all the time? I had no interest in sharing my "forever" girl with whoever.

I told Aja that it was over and that I didn't want to go with her anymore. She said if that's the way I wanted it, then that's the way it would be. She was angry and didn't want to talk to me anymore, and right away I was tripping. I really missed her, and at night, when I thought of her dating other guys, I got so angry I couldn't sleep. After a week of misery I was ready to take her back, but it was too late. My friends laughed at me because I took it so hard. I guess that's what friends are for—to laugh at you.

So my junior high school experience was pretty normal. I dug sports; boxing and basketball became a big part of my life; I was an OK student, making Bs and Cs. Every report card came with the note "Could try harder, needs to apply himself." But at the time I was content to just get by and go under the radar. The one class I really loved was music. The school choir wasn't for me—too geeky—though I did rap and sing in a couple of talent shows. I never won. I just didn't take any of it seriously. I had sports, friends, cute girls, parties and classes. Life was as good as it could get. I was enjoying myself.

Everything was cool. I managed to stay out of trouble and just kept rolling. Me and my crew were gearing up for high school now. But things were rapidly changing in the streets of Los Angeles. I was about to find out just how much.

Chapter II

LAYIN'**DOWN**THE**FOUNDATION**

MY FAVORITE UNCLE IS UNCLE RICKY . . .

. . . AT SEVENTY-SIX, HE'S SEEN EVERYTHING. One of Ricky's favorite sayings is, "If you hang around the barbershop long enough, you're gonna get your hair cut." I always thought it was something cool my uncle would say when the situation called for it, but it never seemed like something that really applied to my own life. As long as I was in elementary or junior high, there wasn't that much bad stuff for me to be influenced by—more just little kid stuff, pranks and teasing. When I got to high school I started to figure out what Ricky meant—that sometimes it's easier to go bad than to stay good, especially when you are surrounded by people who are OK with going bad themselves.

High school was a whole new world. I felt like I had been spit out of a cool little world, and into a rough and ugly one. About a week into school Uncle Ricky's barbershop saying finally caught up with me. I realized that no matter what kind of person you want to be, your surroundings are going to affect you. Or even better—if you hang around negative stuff long enough, it's going to rub off on you sooner or later. Guilty by association. The bottom line is that high school turned out to be one big, dangerous trip. Most people go through a lot of changes in high school. It's part of the deal. But the changes I saw were so radical it was like there was a different game altogether going on. Everything was all of a sudden more serious. A lot more serious. It seemed sometimes like there

was pure evil roaming the streets of Los Angeles.

My junior high experience felt pretty much kind of carefree and fun. I know it wasn't that way for everybody, but I had a good time. High school was another matter, though. Maybe it was the school I went to—Hamilton. Or it was that area of Los Angeles. Maybe it was that time in history. It was probably a combination of all of those things. In the two years between '97 and '99, things got a lot wilder for a whole lot of people I knew. Things got rougher and crazier. It seems like between graduating from junior high, hanging for the summer, and entering high school in the fall, things got serious and took a really weird turn.

When I was younger we'd hear about people getting in trouble, getting arrested, getting killed, but it was always far away enough that it didn't seem that real, or that bad. Now people I knew, the little homies I'd grown up with, were becoming darker and much more aggressive. You'd hear about beat downs—a whole gang of people taking down one guy—every day. Everybody was carrying weapons. Every other person was on the corner slinging dope. Everybody seemed to have an attack dog. Everybody seemed to be angry, and there seemed to be no kind of positive outlet for that energy. Fun had been taken out of the equation. It got so that even simple things, like wearing the wrong clothes or stepping into the wrong neighborhood, had life-or-death consequences. People were mobbin', hurting each other and even dying. And nobody, at least nobody in my end of town, got a free pass. It affected everybody I knew. It was like a chain reaction of bad things happening. Everybody was acting like they automatically had a license to trip. Everybody wanted to play gangsta.

You had to watch, or at least be aware of, every move you made, because somebody, somewhere along the line was going to have a beef about something or other. The kind of violence going down on a bs level was amazing. People were getting beat down, stabbed up and even shot up over the stupidest stuff you could imagine. There was a lot of random hating going on. It seemed like not a day would pass without me hearing about somebody I knew getting hurt or getting in trouble. It was ill.

And everything was worse if you were any kind of loner. If you didn't have some kind of backup—like big brothers or a group of friends—you were an easy target. You had to bond together in a group just for your own self-protection. This was some serious business happening. As far as school went, learning came in second. Survival won—hands down. That was my major in high school—survival.

Looking back on it, I wish I had been a different kind of student. I really wasn't a school-driven kid. It wasn't like I was a problem kid or a bad student. I was just, well, like a lot of kids my age—being a teenager. You know how that is. It ain't the easiest job in the world, but everybody works it for a few years. You think you know everything there is to know. But reality rolls in and you find out real quick that you don't really know anything. I guess that's part of growing up—finding out that you really don't know it all. In school I only read enough or studied enough to get passing grades. Now I make sure to read something every day. I love reading. It opens you up to all kinds of new ideas. I can't learn enough, and I'm happy about that.

I think I was lucky to have a family who cared about me. A lot of my friends were pretty much on their own from a young age—most of them were like me and didn't have fathers—but I figured I was blessed with having a mother and grandmother who wouldn't let me get away with anything. The few times I came close to crossing the line, they were on me like gravy on grits. Looking back, I can see how frightening it was for them, and how hard it must have been knowing they couldn't offer me anything better.

IT AFFECTED EVERYBODY I KNEW. IT WAS LIKE A CHAIN REACTION OF BAD THINGS HAPPENING. EVERYBODY WAS ACTING LIKE THEY AUTOMATICALLY HAD A LICENSE TO TRIP. EVERYBODY WANTED TO PLAY GANGSTA.

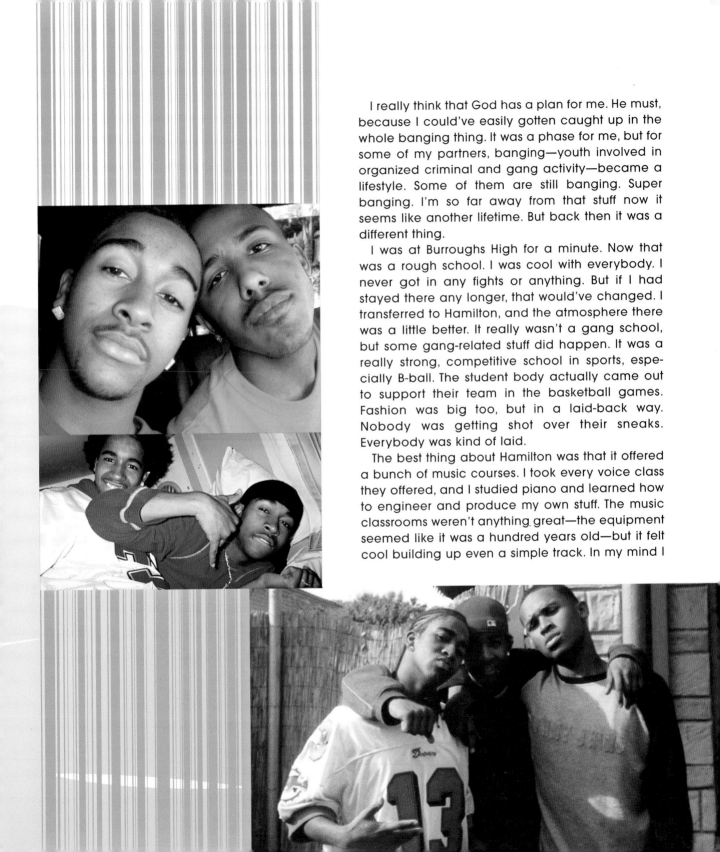

I really think that God has a plan for me. He must, because I could've easily gotten caught up in the whole banging thing. It was a phase for me, but for some of my partners, banging—youth involved in organized criminal and gang activity—became a lifestyle. Some of them are still banging. Super banging. I'm so far away from that stuff now it seems like another lifetime. But back then it was a different thing.

I was at Burroughs High for a minute. Now that was a rough school. I was cool with everybody. I never got in any fights or anything. But if I had stayed there any longer, that would've changed. I transferred to Hamilton, and the atmosphere there was a little better. It really wasn't a gang school, but some gang-related stuff did happen. It was a really strong, competitive school in sports, especially B-ball. The student body actually came out to support their team in the basketball games. Fashion was big too, but in a laid-back way. Nobody was getting shot over their sneaks. Everybody was kind of laid.

The best thing about Hamilton was that it offered a bunch of music courses. I took every voice class they offered, and I studied piano and learned how to engineer and produce my own stuff. The music classrooms weren't anything great—the equipment seemed like it was a hundred years old—but it felt cool building up even a simple track. In my mind I could hear what it would sound like with real musicians, and me singing over them.

I didn't really think of myself as a singer at this point. I mean I was singing, but to myself mostly, in the shower or when I was walking home. I hadn't made the leap of thinking that I could do something as amazing as becoming a recording artist. To be honest, I didn't really have any idea what I wanted to do when I graduated. I was just happy to be getting by without too much trouble from the rougher kids.

So my high school life went on, and I tried to make it as normal as possible, but around the edges there was still this feeling that at any moment things could turn ugly.

Sometimes it's hard to explain how rough our neighborhood was for us. If you didn't live it, you can't really understand what it's like to have the threat of violence hanging over you all the time, even in stupid, everyday situations. My best friend in tenth grade was this kid called Michael McGee, and we used to eat at the Burger King not far from my house all the time. All of the way through elementary school and junior high, me and Big Mike (he really wasn't that much bigger than I was) would fight with each other on a regular basis. We'd be whipping up on each other for just about anything. I think we thought that if we acted tough, we'd look tough, and maybe we'd look just tough enough to keep the older, dangerous kids away. No matter how bad our fights were, we were always friends the next day. We needed each other, for safety as well as friendship, something I learned at Burger King.

On this particular day Mike and I were ordering a couple of burgers when a group of guys fell in behind us. There was maybe eight or nine of them. I could tell a couple of those guys had to be hitting twenty or even older. Me and McGee are like fourteen. They started loud talking about what they were going to do to us when we got outside. Now, we had never seen these dudes before, and we didn't have any kind of beef with them, but that didn't make any difference. They had plans for us. Random evil. "I'm gonna bust this kid up so bad his

momma won't even want him back." "He won't be munching on any more burgers when he don't have teeth." I couldn't believe it, all me and McGee wanted was to eat our food. We didn't know these guys, so what was their problem with us?

Now, I can take care of myself with all of the boxing I had been doing. Michael could scrap too. We weren't no punks. But these guys were much bigger and older guys, and there was a lot of them. We couldn't have done anything with all of them except maybe get stomped or get our teeth knocked out. Or worse.

Michael and I got our bags of takeout and started easing out of the door. As soon as we went outside, these guys came after us. We did the only thing we could do—we broke. We took off, boning out hard, and these guys were right on us. We ran a couple of blocks at full speed, and a few of them were keeping up with us. They must've wanted us bad. I don't know why. Some of the guys chasing us—the real big ones—got winded and gave up. Being chased by three or four dudes is better than being chased by ten. Still, I knew that if we got snatched, the slow ones would eventually catch up and be in on the beat down.

We kept running hard. Mike and I were talking to each other as we're running. "Cut down here!" "Turn right up ahead!" The guys chasing us were still yelling out threats. The more we ran, the madder they got. Mike stumbled a bit, but it was just enough to let the guy behind us catch right up on him. Without breaking stride, I pivoted and hurled my bag of Burger King right into this guy's face. Bull's-eye! That felt good—just like delivering a knockout punch. The hot fries must have hurt, 'cuz he stumbled off of the pavement and ended up falling

1   Q: Superman or Batman?

    A: Superman. Batman's got a lot of cool gadgets, but Superman is a very special kind of hero. He's got superpowers. I identify with special individuals.

2   Q: Hot dogs or hamburgers?

    A: Hot dogs.

3   Q: Comedy or action movies?

    A: Both. I'm leaning toward comedy.

4   Q: Shaq or Kobe?

    A: Kobe. Kobe makes the plays. I played point guard, too.

5   Q: Malcolm or Martin?

    A: A draw. They were both great men. I wish there were more like them.

6   Q: Biggie or Tupac?

    A: Tupac.

7   Q: Dogs or cats?

    A: Dogs. I have American terriers a.k.a. pit bulls.

8   Q: Favorite holiday?

    A: My birthday. That's a holiday, right?

9   Q: Favorite destination outside of the U.S.A.?

    A: I've never been there, but I'm looking at warm weather, white sand and water—Saint-Tropez.

10 Q: Dream car?

    A: Right now, the Hummer.

into a bunch of trash cans. Michael and I hit the high gear and were gone.

Taking their fastest man out of the chase gave us just enough time to get away. We ran and hid in the back of this Catholic school. We stayed there for a while because those dudes were still trippin'. They were really mad now and were still cruising the neighborhood looking for us. From our hiding place we could see them, but they couldn't see us. Mike still had his Burger King bag. He started to eat, and I asked for half of his sandwich.

He turned to me and said, "No, you shouldn't have thrown yours away." I couldn't believe that crap. I had just saved his ass, and he had the nerve to come up with that! We started scrapping right then

and there. The food hit the ground, and we stepped all over it as we were struggling. The burgers were squashed under our sneakers, and the ketchup exploded all over the floor. We had to stop fighting and laugh about it. The next day we were partners again. That's just the kind of friends we were.

The one thing to come out of our narrow escape was that I realized I should be hanging tough with a network of people, if for no other reason than to stay safe. I really didn't need to be getting chased through my own neighborhood by a bunch of strangers. The whole time Mike and I were running, I was thinking "This is some bull———." I was determined that that was going to be the last time that kind of mess happened.

When I was at Hamilton, gang culture was really popular throughout the city. In L.A., there were Crips, Bloods and like a hundred varieties of each gang rolling around the city. The Crips are blue and the Bloods are red. The differences, the way I understand it, don't go much deeper than that. For years these two groups fought each other—and themselves—constantly over territory and whatever else they could find to beef about. After the L.A. riots of '92, the whole Crips and Bloods killing-each-other-off thing cooled down a lot. There's still a lot of banging going on, but now it's about drugs, money and all of that kind of stuff.

Me and my friends were never into that whole Crips or Bloods—which one to join—thing. We were all from the same neighborhood, and we didn't have much in common with either group. We just kind of formed up to watch each other's backs—especially in our own neighborhood. It started out as one thing and quickly became something else. We even gave ourselves a name—Under Age Criminals. UAC—the name says it all. We knew that we were just too cool.

All gangs start out the same way—as a means to protect their members. We didn't start out thinking that we were going to be the violent ones; we thought we were going to protect ourselves from violence. Somehow that changed.

At first the UAC didn't have any kind of identity or anything. We were just together. We didn't have any special colors or signs. We were just there watching out for each other and putting people on when the situation called for it. Nobody was going to take advantage of us if we could do something about it.

Some of my pals from early childhood were still in the mix. Lovell was in. He was quiet, but you didn't want to get on his wrong side, because he could throw down. In elementary school, he was fighting junior high dudes and whipping them. I actually saw him knock a couple of guys out. He'd put somebody out, and the rest of us would look at each other in disbelief and go, "How does he do that?" Lovell had no fear. Our pal Boner was in with us too. Boner was the Hispanic kid who was down with the brothers. He could hang. He was another one who wasn't scared of anything. My cousin

WITHOUT BREAKING STRIDE, I PIVOTED AND HURLED MY BAG OF BURGER KING RIGHT INTO THIS GUY'S FACE. BULL'S-EYE! THAT FELT GOOD—JUST LIKE DELIVERING A KNOCKOUT PUNCH. THE HOT FRIES MUST HAVE HURT, 'CUZ HE STUMBLED OFF OF THE PAVEMENT AND ENDED UP FALLING INTO A BUNCH OF TRASH CANS.

Jovan was tough and ready. Big Mike McGee smashed with us too.

So our members were basically good kids who were just watching each other's backs; that changed when Kevin joined. Kevin and his brother Keith were like a year apart. Keith was a normal dude, but Kevin was super duper hard. At first it was cool having him on our side, because he was so fierce you couldn't imagine losing with him around. Pretty soon, though, he got kind of weird. Kevin turned into a real vulture. He wasn't into showing mercy or thinking a problem through. He would always go for the most direct solution to any problem—violence. I don't know if he enjoyed being violent or if he just didn't know how to be any other way; he had had a rough childhood, but so had Keith, and Keith wasn't crazy.

The only person who could control Kevin was his brother, but it quickly got to the point where even Keith couldn't control him. Meanwhile other things were changing with the UAC. We'd always avoided adopting colors because that wasn't what we were about, then one day Keith showed

up with a dozen brown bandannas. Suddenly we were a gang for real.

Adopting colors was the first sign that we were on the wrong track. We would have our brown rags in our back pockets, and we'd hit up every car that came by. "Where you from?!?" We'd throw up our signs, and if they didn't hit us back, there was going to be some trouble. If they wanted to stop and discuss the matter, we had something for them. In a short period of time we went from watching out for each other to challenging unfamiliar faces that came through our neighborhood.

I guess we were starting to get pretty cocky; we were running our hood, or so it seemed. Then word came down from an older, more established gang nearby that we needed to slow down. Our response was simple: "Whatever. You want to see us? You know where to find us!" Older or younger, it didn't matter. When we were rolling together, a squabble wasn't a big thing. We weren't about to turn down any kind of challenge—no matter who or where it came from.

The Under Age Criminals were starting to get

pretty well known in our neighborhood, but the truth was that we weren't really criminals.

We didn't do break-ins. We didn't jack money or cars. We didn't boost. We didn't sling. We were in it to protect each other and to protect our home base. UAC didn't go out of the way looking for trouble—like going up against a crew from another neighborhood—but when it came to us, we were more than willing to handle it. I didn't know it then, but Uncle Ricky's saying had come to pass—I had stayed in the barbershop too long, and now I was getting my hair cut.

The gang life is crazy, especially in L.A., but it's never going to go away. Being in a gang is a way to show that you're hard. People give you respect in a way that you wouldn't get if you were on your own. And you want to show you're down with everybody. Your peers. A better name for our gang would have been The Missing Daddy Club, 'cuz most of us didn't have fathers. My friends who ended up getting into gangs hard-core found guidance and father figures there. I was just lucky that I had been raised to believe that I did have a dad out there and that one day he would return. Whether my mom believed that or not, it meant a great deal to me. I never had that hole in my heart that my friends did, thinking that their fathers didn't love them enough to want them. Besides, I was the oldest child, and even though I was young, I was like the male head in the house, at least till my dad came back. I could understand what other kids were seeing, though.

Guns weren't a big thing, at least the way I saw it, until 1999. You would always hear about people getting shot, drive-bys and all of that kind of stuff, but all the shootings seemed to happen in other places and to other people. Me and my crew were used to fighting with our fists, but suddenly it seemed like everybody was bringing heat. That changed things a lot. Not everybody wants to get into a fistfight, but anybody can fire a gun. Usually, the type of people who are happy to shoot at you but who are too scared to fight you are the most dangerous of all, 'cuz deep down they are scared. You've got to be a different kind of dude to stand up toe-to-toe with somebody and slug it out.

Everybody out on the streets had a gun now. They were playing for keeps. With guns in the game, things really got serious.

One night a shoot-out went down in front of my house. It was dark, and the whole scene was framed in the living room window. For real, it felt like I was in the cinema, feet jacked up on the seat in front of me, munching on popcorn, watching this madness. The craziest part was that these two dudes were strangers; they didn't have some long-standing beef—they just exchanged a few words, and the shooting began. When the smoke cleared, both of them were on the ground bleeding, and nobody could remember how the whole thing had started. It wasn't about a woman. It wasn't about money. It wasn't about family. It wasn't about drugs. It was about the fact that both of them were carrying guns. That kind of thing was typical. Random evil.

Something started to change inside of me. Boner's older brother, Juan, would show us guns and things. He was a cool dude; he'd been around for a while and knew a little something. He tried to talk us out of getting guns but said he could get them for us if we needed them. I think the day I decided not to get a gun was a big moment in my life. Some part of me was smart enough to know I had a choice in front of me, and that the wrong answer could lead to a bad end for Omari Grandberry. I told Juan I could handle my business and that I didn't need a gun. Of course it would be a while before I was smart enough to get out altogether.

For a minute I was seriously into the Under Age Criminals thing. It was a good thing to feel protected and be a part of something. But the longer we hung, the more we started edging into some real banging. I guess that's just the way things work. If you hang around the barbershop too long. . . . I think people in my family were beginning to suspect something. They were always asking me questions about where I was going or who I was going with. I managed to sidestep most of those questions, but they knew that something was up.

I had faded away from boxing by this time. I would see Coach Johnson on the street every now and then. He would give me that look with that cigar in his mouth and say, "You're screwing up, Grandberry. You know you're screwing up. You know that, don't you?" I'd play ignorant, but he knew what was going on. He'd come back with, "You know what I'm talking about. Don't play stupid with me. You need to get your narrow ass back in that ring and be about something." Then I'd make some excuse to get away. He could really make me feel bad.

Feeling bad for a few minutes didn't matter, though. I felt that what we were doing was for real. The UAC wasn't joking. We formed up first for mutual protection. Then our mission became all about protecting the turf—our territory. Then it became about just being mean and tough. Standing on the corner intimidating strangers seemed like the most logical thing in the world. But the one thing that I didn't buy into was disrespecting women. That became part of the overall tough guy/gang banging thing, but I just wasn't with it. The whole bitch, ho deal is something I couldn't get involved with and won't get involved with. That ain't me. The women in

my life—relatives, teachers, girlfriends and fans—mean too much to me to be just dissing them off-hand. That's not going to happen. Everything else, though, was on the table.

When things got rough for us—the UAC—we stuck together and took it in stride. And there was always some kind of excitement happening around us. One night I was at Boner's house when the cops raided the place. They weren't looking for us, but we ran anyhow. We ran through yards, jumped over fences and eventually got away. We outran the police dogs that night. Sometimes I think that the next step for me was breaking the law. Slinging and jacking wouldn't be a stretch the way that we were going. I'm sure we could've rationalized it easily: "I need some money." Or "I need some clothes." I'm glad it didn't go like that. It could've very easily. But like I said—God has a plan.

Three unrelated things happened that kind of pushed me into another direction away from the UAC. These things didn't happen one on top of the other. It was a gradual thing. First, there was a guy I used to talk to every day at school. He was a cool dude. We used to play basketball sometimes, and I remember that he laughed a lot. One day they

announced over the PA system that he was dead. I was shocked. I had hung out with the guy the day before; him being dead didn't seem real. Apparently he had been playing Russian roulette, and he'd shot himself in the head. What? Russian roulette? Why would anybody with good sense even think about playing that? I had never handled anything like this before, and I didn't like the way the sudden death thing was feeling. The guy had been there what seemed like just a minute ago. And now he was gone. Forever. It was permanent. And the weird thing is that I wasn't even that tight with him. But his death really affected me. The false security that teenagers can get into about being indestructible had suddenly been proven false. Mortality was for real. People, even young people, die and don't come back.

A few months later the UAC crew showed up at my crib. They told me about this guy who they said was talking about my mother. At the time, if you talked about somebody's mother, it was on. I didn't know this guy, and deep down inside I suspected that the accusation was probably false. But I wasn't about to look weak in front of my friends, no matter what the truth of the situation was. I put on my clothes and went over there right away.

I was wearing a brown plaid shirt—my fighting shirt—and I was ready for action. I stood on his stoop and called him out.

"Whatch you saying about my mother?"

"I don't know you, man. Why would I—"

Before the sentence was out of his mouth, I tagged him full on the nose. He reeled back a step, and for good measure I did it again. My crew was hollering by now, telling me to beat this fool down for daring to start it up with me. He was backing up, and he blocked my next punch. My fighting shirt got torn a little, and I really got mad. There was

nothing that was going to save this kid from a good ass-whipping.

The boy's mother was looking out of the window, and she saw what was going down. She ran outside, yelling at us to stop. As soon as they saw her, my crew split. I ran behind the garage thinking I could duck through the alley, but there was a concrete wall that blocked my way. I dived under her Honda Civic, my breath tight in my chest. I didn't want to get called out by some fool's mama. I could see her feet approaching me from under the car. They stopped, and I heard her say, "You get out of there right this instant."

Boy, she was mad. Her hands were on her hips and she was tapping her foot. I knew I was in trouble. I was expecting the police to show up at any moment. Instead, she said, "You want a fight, you can have a fight. My boy's right out front."

I mumbled something like, "Whatever. Let's do it."

I was ready to whale this kid, but he muttered, "I'm not gonna fight him," even when his mother told him to. I even felt kind of bad for making the kid look like a punk in front of his mother. We grudgingly shook hands after that and went our separate ways. I was lucky to avoid catching a charge that day.

Fast-forward a couple of months. I was playing ball in the local gym when something caught my eye. There was a young kid in the ring, and he was looking good. He was smooth and confident, throwing punches and moving like a professional. Even though it had been months since I'd been in the ring, I could still appreciate someone with talent. I stopped to watch him and thought to myself, "Who is this? Sugar Ray Leonard?" I knew his opponent from my days with Coach Johnson, and I remembered he was a tough little dude with serious skills. This new guy that he was boxing was making him look bad, though. He was landing seri-

ous shots and not taking any in return. I just had to stand there and watch.

When the bell rang I walked up to the ring to catch a better look at the new kid, but when he pulled off his headgear I saw it was the kid from the fight, the one whose mother had tried to get us to fight.

My mouth was wide open. This guy had some seriously sweet moves. He was lightning fast—faster than I was—and he had some real punching power. After the first match he went up against a couple of other kids, and he outclassed, outpunched, outmaneuvered and outfought them all. The truth of that moment was kind of devastating; it was apparent that if we had fought that day out on the street, he would've kicked my ass. Totally. I realized that he'd done me a big favor by not accepting my challenge. I guess this guy was one of those reluctant warriors who only fights when it is necessary, and then he fights for keeps. He felt that he didn't have to prove anything to anybody—not even his mother. I had made the mistake of judging that book by its cover, and, man, had I been wrong. He waved at me as I was leaving. We both knew what was up. On the way home I remembered how confident and cocky I had been about going up against this kid. I'd figured he was a punk for not stepping up, and that he'd been scared of me. I'd thought I was the powerful, strong person, but I had been a hundred percent wrong. This kid could have wiped the street with me, and he'd known it, and his mother had known it; the only person who hadn't known it was me. This really shook me up—if I could have been so wrong about this, what else was I wrong about?

The third thing happened at school. I had been singing and rapping at talent shows at Hamilton

∽ TOP 10 FAVORITE MOVIES ∽

FAVORITE FILMS TO ME ARE MOVIES THAT YOU SEE MORE THAN ONCE. SOMETIMES EVEN THREE OR FOUR TIMES. IN NO PARTICULAR ORDER >

1. The Five Heartbeats
2. The Matrix (the first one)
3. Braveheart
4. Lord of the Rings: The Fellowship of the Ring
   Lord of the Rings: The Two Towers
   Lord of the Rings: The Return of the King
5. Remember the Titans
6. Gladiator
7. Bad Boys (the first one)
8. The Passion of the Christ
9. Beverly Hills Cop (the first one)
10. You Got Served

BONUS PICK >

11. High Noon

It's old. It's black and white. It's a Western. But I could really identify with what the hero was going through. Check it out.

since I started there. I didn't take it very seriously—it was just something to do for an hour or so.

One day me and a few other guys from my music class cut out of class and were singing in the stairwell at the back of the school. We liked singing on this particular stairwell because the sound would echo up and down the flights of stairs, giving our voices a cool reverby effect. We pretty much lost ourselves in the slow jam we were singing, hitting it like R. Kelly with a bit of old-time harmony thrown in. We were just goofing, basically. Regular classes were going on, but we didn't think anyone would hear our singing. Then Mr. Giles, our gym teacher, walked up on us. I remember Mr. Giles as being kind of mean in the way he dealt with students, but when he saw us he didn't say anything; he just kicked back and kind of smiled. We didn't know what to make of that, so we kept singing. When we

finished the song, he told us that it was time to go back to the cafeteria. Not in the mean way he usually came off with—in fact, he even complimented us on the way we sounded and told us that we reminded him of when he was a kid and the older boys on his block would sing doo-wops on the street corners and in apartment stairwells. He told us to keep up with our singing, and I found that kind of encouraging. I think that was one of the first times I realized that my music could change people and make them feel something. Still, it wasn't something I was taking seriously at that point.

These three situations changed me, and all of a sudden I just wasn't as into the Under Age Criminals as I had been. It was like a light slowly dawning in my mind. I'd seen close-up how life could be snatched away in an instant, and how the closer you walked to the thug life, the better your chances of dying a thug death. It was that simple. If the kid who shot himself hadn't had access to a gun, hadn't seen them flashed around by other kids, he'd probably still be alive. That was a heavy lesson. Once you pull the trigger, the bullet ain't going back into the gun. You are committed.

Second, having the good fortune not to have that kid kick my ass out on the street when he clearly could have let me know something important—especially as it relates to banging. No matter how tough you think you are, there is always someone tougher. Keep messing around, and one day you will find him.

But the most important thing that happened was realizing I could do something to a stranger just through the power of my voice. It was hard to express to my friends, but the look on Mr. Giles's face as our singing took him back to another time and place stayed with me. I knew he had gone back to a time when he was young and happy just through listening to our music. If you could have seen what a mean old guy he was, you'd understand just how amazing the lost look on his face was!

So slowly I pulled away from the Under Age Criminals. It didn't happen all at once, but instead of hanging 24/7, I'd start to chill on my own every now and then, until gradually the "now and then" was every day. I really believe that the decisions you make early on are going to determine what happens for the rest of your life.

My decision to step back from the Under Age Criminal vortex when I did changed my life. If things had gone any other way, I could still be hanging today. I can't believe now that I was doing some of that dangerous, misguided stuff we were doing. Fighting for no reason. Intimidating people. I look back on it now and I see that it was all bull. A complete and dangerous waste of time. I could've really hurt someone out there—and I could've gotten hurt. You see all of these young brothers riding around in wheelchairs and you know what I mean.

We did a B2K concert once where there was a whole section close to the stage of young guys in wheelchairs. It was probably twenty-five or thirty of them. We thought it was MS or a cerebral palsy group until they told us that they were all gunshot victims. We couldn't believe it. I went like, "Damn!

THIS KID COULD HAVE WIPED THE STREET WITH ME, AND HE'D KNOWN IT, AND HIS MOTHER HAD KNOWN IT; THE ONLY PERSON WHO HADN'T KNOWN IT WAS ME. THIS REALLY SHOOK ME UP—IF I COULD HAVE BEEN SO WRONG ABOUT THIS, WHAT ELSE WAS I WRONG ABOUT?

How did things come to this?" My heart went out to those guys. They were young, and they were going to be confined to those chairs for the rest of their lives. The image of those guys stays with me.

My aunt Monyee kept trying to get me to come with her to Chris Stokes's place—this music manager on Colfax. This was happening around the same time that my interest in UAC was fading. She and Chris had been dating, and I think she insisted that I go with her because she knew that these streets were about to cause me some trouble. Taking me along and showing me another side of life was her way of staging an intervention.

The first time I met Chris and some of his artists was heavy. I'd never met people who were really doing it, forging careers, making money in the music business. It was an eye-opener, just as my aunt intended.

Chris and my aunt introduced me to Marques Houston and the Immature crew and let me hang out at recording sessions, rehearsals and even some of their live shows. I was starting to see close-up how the music business actually worked.

That up-close look at how some people roll just reinforced things for me. Mobbin' and that whole UAC lifestyle just wasn't working anymore. There was a whole lot more to life, and it was happening right in front of me. I just couldn't see it until the time was right.

Even now I'm still bugging when I think about that whole thug life thing. I hear about people I grew up with and what they're into now, and some of it's cool. A lot of it is sad.

There was a guy I went to elementary school with that we called Domo. We grew apart in junior high. That was the time he started banging hard. Domo never quit. He mapped out his course early. He kept upping his game. He kept playing the streets harder. He kept coming with it. Other guys were trying to drop out, but Domo got into some super banging. That's SUPER BANGING! Now he's gone. Somebody shot him. That was inevitable the way he was carrying it.

Anthony (Boner) was running the streets hard too, but thankfully he now has a daughter and he has turned his life around. He even named his little girl after me—Omarion—and asked me to be her godfather. She's my heart—only two years old but with a wonderful personality already emerging. It's amazing how Anthony's whole way of thinking got switched around when she came along. I know it isn't always easy for him, but he has done an amazing job carving out a life for his daughter. It makes me proud of him. Me? I can't tell you how happy I am to be away from all of that noise. Words can't describe it. I might even write a song about it one day. By freeing myself of that gang mentality, I was finally able to allow myself to see things in a different way. To think in a different way. I was allowing myself to become creative again. Creative like I was when I was a kid. When I was much younger, my imagination could take me anywhere that I wanted to go. I even imagined myself performing in front of an arena-size audience a couple of times. But when I hit my teenage years, it was all about being tough and surviving. The imagination and the creativity that I was born with suddenly got left out of the picture. I believe that everybody is creative one way or another—and if you let God's plan work itself out, then you don't need all of that other madness in your life. Serious banging equals madness. There is an alternative way. You've just got to listen to what life is telling you. It's all about listening. Not many people know how to do that. It seems like a whole lot of people are too busy talking, to listen.

Chapter III

THE**DRESS**REHEARSAL

I WAS READY FOR SOMETHING TO HAPPEN.

B2K WAS "DISCOVERED" AT AN EPIC RECORDS SHOWCASE. Getting to that point where we were "discovered" and became an overnight success story took some time and some real hard work.

Like I said, I met Chris Stokes through my auntie, Monyee. She and Chris were dating then, and they're happily married now. I had actually spent some time with him as a kid—when I was around eight or nine she would take me over to Chris's house on Detroit Place in mid-city. It was a cool place to hang out. Chris was into the music management game, and he was always putting these different groups together. Girl groups. Mixed groups. Kiddie groups. His breakthrough group and the most successful was Immature. They grew up and in a few years became the best-selling IMX. So I was around some cool people at an early age. Chris's spot was the place to be.

Of course once high school and the UAC came along, I stopped going with her for a while. I was sixteen when I started hanging with Chris again. My aunt had let it drop that Chris was looking for a lead singer in another group he was putting together. I thought, "Why not? At the very least, it's something to do."

This was New Year's Eve 2000. I was supposed to hang out with my boys in the neighborhood that night, but for some reason I changed my mind even before my aunt called. I just wasn't feeling it that night. There was no special lady in the picture at the moment, but I wasn't sweating that either. I was ready for something to happen. I was ready for something new. This would be the first time in a couple of years that I had been out with my aunt.

We went up to Chris's crib up on Colfax Boulevard in Studio City. There was always energy and activity going on at Chris's place. It was a place where a lot of young artists and entertainers hung. The creativity was bouncing off the walls. On some nights one group would be rehearsing out in the garage. Another would be listening to tracks in another area. Somebody would be baking something in the kitchen. Another set of folks would be in another room writing songs and composing music. The place seemed to be always buzzing with excitement. The people there were sharpening their skills as they got to know each other. We came to call this place the Colfax House.

Around ten o'clock, Monyee and I arrived at the house on Colfax. Chris was having a party that

35

night, and that's where I met Druex Fredrick (Lil' Fizz), De Mario Thornton (Raz-B) and Jarell Houston (J-Boog). I recognized Raz because, ironically, he and I went to the same school. We were friendly toward each other, but we really didn't hang; still, it was cool to see each other, and we started talking. Turns out Raz, Fizz and J-Boog were in a singing group with two other guys. They called themselves Melodic, but it wasn't working out for them. They were dissolving that group and were looking for another lead. Raz knew I could sing a little bit from around the school, and finally he asked me, "So, you singing with anybody right now?" I didn't think he was serious, so I just replied, "I'm not really a singer, it's just something I do for fun."

The funny thing was that even as we sat on Chris's couch and kicked it I felt an instant camaraderie with the other three. It's like we just clicked and understood each other. They felt it too, and I found out later on that they all decided right then that they wanted me to come in as the lead vocalist.

It was getting later and the party was getting looser, and at one point a couple of people got up and performed. The performances were tight. Suddenly Chris turns to me and says, "Omari, free-style for a minute." I'm like, "What is this? An audition or something?" and that's exactly what it turned out to be, albeit an unplanned one. I could see that Chris had something on his mind, so I cut loose with a couple of steps. The music was working, and almost without any thought I improvised for a minute.

Next Chris put on another track, then Raz, Fizz and Jarell performed. I remember saying, "Wow!" out loud. They were really, really good. I was down with everything they were doing. I could read their energy and felt that it was corresponding to mine. Then, when they were finished, Chris asked me to get up and sing. I had originally wanted to be a rapper. A couple of years earlier Chris had told me that I should be singing. He said that anybody can rap. Singing is an art. And he'd thought that I had it. I'd taken his advice and given singing a try. I'd thought I'd sounded okay for talent shows at the rec center. But now it seemed like all of a sudden I was being whisked off to another level. The audition had gotten real.

I was out on the floor now singing my heart out. I was going for it. At one point the other three guys jumped in, and we did an impromptu couple of steps. I was starting to feel some chemistry happen. We're the same height. The same weight. All of us could move. I was feeling this. The routine was totally made up—but it looked good. It must've worked, because just then Chris came off the sofa and said, "That's it! That's the group." I was pumped,

IT'S LIKE WE JUST CLICKED AND UNDERSTOOD EACH OTHER. THEY FELT IT TOO, AND I FOUND OUT LATER ON THAT THEY ALL DECIDED RIGHT THEN THAT THEY WANTED ME TO COME IN AS THE LEAD VOCALIST.

and so were the guys—Chris might have been family, but he wasn't going to bs us if he didn't think we were good. His excitement was for real.

Suddenly, right there in the living room of the Colfax House, I felt a flood of positive energy swamping me. It was like a sleeping entertainment gene was waking up inside of me. That gene is in my bloodline. Some families have a criminal gene or a military gene that they pass on. We've got the entertainment thing going on. I've got musicians, singers and dancers on both sides of my family. My younger brother O'Ryan has it too. It's hereditary. My whole natural energy is like that of an entertainer. I would always sing and dance around the house or whenever I got the chance. I never took any of it seriously, though—that is, until the moment of our first performance. It was like a transforming moment. A new door had opened, and I was now looking into the future. I liked what I was seeing.

My aunt, Monyee, was all excited. Even though it was almost two in the morning, she called my mom and asked if she thought I would be interested in being the lead singer of an up-and-coming group. She explained that this wasn't a garage band or playground group but a crew with some serious potential and some serious management firepower behind it. My mom gave her blessings and said that she would see how I felt about it. She

would ask me. She didn't have to ask. I was already there.

When I finally got home, my mom and I sat down and talked about it for real. I was underage, so she had to sign on and agree to my being in the band. I had no idea what would happen with the band, but I was thinking that it would be a cool idea to be a part of a crew, as opposed to going on the road by myself—if it got that far. It would be much better to have three other people that you are cool with and can fun with. I really don't like to be alone for too long—like I say, I've always been part of a group, be it the UAC or B2K. It's not like I'm going to freak out or anything if I'm left alone, but ever since I was little I never liked being alone. I could never figure out why I was like that. It just was. Being part of a four-man crew was going to be a good thing. Even if the group never made it, at least I wouldn't be alone and away from home. But all that I was thinking was that this was a good thing. I saw this as a win-win situation.

I was a little concerned about the fact that I never had any formal training in singing and dancing, but Chris didn't see it that way. We sat down over lunch one day and he said, "O, I go by my gut. You're rough, but that's cool. I know you've got it." I guess I was still worried about it, because he went on, "You know I can't promise you anything. You've

got raw talent, and I see opportunities for you. If everybody does their part, there's a shot you all could go far. That's more than most people have in this business."

Like I say, Chris is mad cool. Soon as we finished our conversation, I felt better about things. I liked the way that that sounded. We all did, and knowing that Chris thought we had it made us all take what he said seriously. Course every band needs a name, and Chris had that figured out too. B2K— Boys of the New Millennium. Since we came together in the first minutes of a brand-new century, I thought the name was dope. It captured what we were all about—newness and excitement.

The very next day—January 2—we started going to regular rehearsals and practices. Sometimes it felt like that was all we did. Learn, rehearse, get better. Nobody minded. We were all into it.

The place we used to rehearse in was actually the garage behind the Colfax House. That garage was like our lab. Our spot. That's the place where we'd try out different moves and work them into routines. The space was set up with a Trinity keyboard, a comfortable couch, and a PC beat machine. There were floor-to-ceiling mirrors along one wall. It was a perfect atmosphere in which our creativity could flourish. We ended up using most everything we came up with, 'cuz it seemed like all the ideas were hot. After a few months we were pretty much living in the lab, and the garage was like the best place in the world to hang and trade off ideas.

I had to play a little catch-up, because Raz, Fizz and Jarell were already used to dancing in tight choreography and I was not a choreographed dancer; I was a street dancer. Dancing had always come naturally to me, and I'd never really wanted lessons; I would go to the little kiddie clubs and do my thing but nothing that was really organized. Let me tell you, it's hard to get in synch with three other people! To master this type of performing, you have to count, dance and watch what is happening all at the same time. Instead of focusing on one thing, I now had to split my concentration and work on several things

simultaneously. Add singing and harmony to the mix, and that's a lot of precision to master. None of that mattered, though. I knew this was a huge opportunity for me, and if I messed it up, I might never have another one. I practiced all hours of the day until eventually I turned things around and got on the same level with the other guys.

As hard as the singing and dancing were, just fitting in with the other guys was even harder at first. When I first joined up, I felt like the outsider in the crew because the other three were already cool with each other; because of their brief time together in Melodic, their relationships had already been established. It was kind of hard for me at first; I wanted to be embraced and be a full-fledged member of the crew. I started doing things out of my character to be accepted—stupid things like telling a bad joke or trying too hard to be heard. One day I insisted on buying lunch for everybody, then ran out of money and had to borrow from Raz.

But the more we worked and hung out together, the less need there was for me to try too hard. Things just started falling into place. Everybody started hanging out together—in the lab, at the Colfax House and out in public. We became like inseparable. Events, concerts, eating places—if you saw one of us, you saw all of us. We turned out to have a lot in common—especially a sense of humor. We'd find ourselves laughing at the same things. People-watching gave us our best laughs.

This period of artistic development was cool 'cuz it was all about being creative. The four of us would practice our singing and harmonies every day, and I could feel us getting better and better. Dave Scott was always around and working with us. Dave was a dancer for another group that Chris had put together a few years back; now he was breaking away and on the path to becoming a first-rate choreographer. I admired the fact that Dave was a self-taught street dancer who'd made the leap to professional choreographer—he was good, one of the best as far as I'm concerned. We were like his first students, and he really worked with us, developing just for us hot moves that no one

had seen before. Then he would take the additional moves that we came up with and refine them. We all had a great working relationship.

In the Colfax House living room there was a big-screen TV that we could see our reflection in when it was turned off. When we needed a break from the lab, we would go to the house to relax and watch TV, and we would end up rehearsing in front of the screen instead. We were the living room kings, and this was our performance space. When company came over we would always perform for them. Chris would ask, "Do you want to see the boys perform?" and then we'd do our thing. He was putting word of mouth into play. Destiny's Child came over, and we did it for them. We were tight with 3LW, and we performed for them too. We always got a positive reception. We made a lot of good friends in the business early on through our living room performances.

Around that time I got tight with Marques Houston. Marques was always at the Colfax House, almost like an artist-in-residence. The four of us in B2K hung out with IMX and got to see and experience a lot of stuff through them. Me and Marques just kind of fit. It turns out that he always wanted a younger brother, and I had always wanted an older

brother. He became just like one. Besides helping me out professionally—with the singing, dancing and stage presence—he also talked to me about all of the other important things that were going on behind the scenes of a career in show business. He told me about friends who had got messed up by the weird things that can go down when you're in the spotlight; he warned me that there would be distractions and pitfalls and about all the other obstacles that can pop up when you start to make it. Marques really warned me about money and that I had to be careful not to land in a situation where it ended up controlling me. I remember specifically one night he said, "You know that there are going to be a whole lot of women coming after you." I was kind of macking it. I said something like, "Bring 'em on!" Then he came back with, "This is one thing that you can't fake. It's great for the ego to have women coming out of the woodwork after you. But you can't lose your focus, and you can't ever put yourself into a situation where you are just using women and discarding them. You wouldn't want anybody to play your mother or sisters like that, would you?" That hit home. I got the message. We'd talk like that all of the time. He would never lecture me. We would talk like brothers. We still do. A lot of people still think we're brothers.

At the time, Marques's band, IMX, was starting to hit it hard—they were becoming very popular and selling a lot of records. We would go everywhere with them, including their rehearsals and recording sessions. We were getting a close-up view of what the future was to hold for us. Some of the rehearsal sessions were off the hook. You had us, IMX and some professional dancers all doing these really cool choreographed and freestyle moves. At some point during the night, someone would play a thumping track that didn't have the IMX vocals yet. We would all get down wherever we were and just dance until we fell out. It was a lot of fun, and we were really getting our act together. We were a team now, and we could really get our dance on.

After months and months of rehearsal, we got really, really good. Every day we seemed to grow a little tighter as a unit. Chris felt that now we were ready to scout out a record label deal. We were confident and hungry, and we kept insisting that Dave make the dancing more difficult—we wanted the challenge of some complicated moves that would really test us. Every time Dave amped up the steps, we threw it right back at him. One day we were working out in the garage, going over the same routine for several hours. The moves were finally falling into place, and I was on automatic. My mind wandered for a minute, and when my concentration snapped back, I looked in the mirror. The first thing I saw was the four of us spinning through a series of real fast and complicated leaping steps. My first thought was, "Whoa! Look at those guys!" And then, "Oh, wait a minute—that's us." I was really impressed with what was happening in the mirror, even if I was in the middle of it.

We all were feeling good about where this thing was going. We had the moves, the music and the identity; we were B2K, and we were finally ready for the world. We all felt that we had something good going on; the trick now was to find a record label that could see what we were all about.

We were pursuing the labels and getting turned down left and right. Every time, the reasons were different, but it all added up to the same thing—"No thanks!" We got all kinds of crazy reasons why we wouldn't make it, like, "Where's the demographic?" "Singing and dancing are dead. Rap is king." "Solo performers are in. Groups are out." "Girl groups are happening. Boy groups are through." What? I don't

really know what the problem was, but one thing I've learned in show business is that nobody knows anything. In other words, no one can tell you with any kind of certainty whether or not an act will be a hit or not.

Everybody pretends to know everything, but nobody really knows anything. It's all a guess. We were back in L.A. and starting to feel a little discouraged; the excitement of the tour had worn off, and everything was back to usual. Maybe we just weren't as good as we thought we were. The only thing that kept us going through this period was each other; we pretty much took turns playing cheerleader and keeping each other pumped. One of us would be dragging and pissed off one day, and the other guys would prop him up and talk him through it. The next day it would be another one of us down, and the other three would keep him going. I'm a pretty positive guy, but I've got to admit that I was starting to feel down too. How come the record executives couldn't see what me and the rest of the guys could clearly see and feel? What was up with that??

Finally Tse Williams, the manager of 3LW, came to see us at Colfax House and was totally knocked out by us. She promised to make some phone calls on our behalf; a meeting was set up with Max Gouse, an executive at Epic. Tse arranged a private showcase for us at his label. Before we went in to perform, Chris took us in a huddle and told us, "Just kick back and remember everything you

꩜ TELL A JOKE ꩜

A bad joke (is there any other kind?):

Man #1: Knock. Knock. Man #2: Get away from my door, you idiot!

love about what you do. If he sees the passion, you'll have a deal."

In all honesty, I was more nervous than I had been on tour or with the other record labels. I had felt pretty much invincible before we did the rounds trying to get a deal. The rejection had made me realize failure was possible—and that was frightening. As you can imagine, we sang like our lives depended on it. Afterwards Max said he couldn't believe that we hadn't been signed yet. He kept saying over and over again, "You guys could be huge."

Pretty much before we were done Max was on the phone to New York arranging for us to fly in and visit the label—and less than a day later we were on a United Airlines flight from the West Coast. On the plane we agreed that this was going to be it. We had been together close to a year and a half

now. That was a year and a half of constant hard work. Everybody was getting frustrated. It was time now for something to happen. Chris was straight with us once again. He told us that he had just about exhausted all of his contacts, and if this didn't come through, then it was over. We had a lot—everything, really—riding on this trip.

The first thing we did after we landed was meet Dave Scott and go over some new steps. After we had those down, we broke out the one stage outfit that we owned—our "official B2K outfit," a matching black pants and shirt thing—but we made sure that we looked sharp. Then we hailed two cabs and booked it over to the SIR studios to audition.

I don't really know who I expected to see, but the first person I noticed when we pulled up was Mr. Tommy Mottola, the Big Man. Tommy Mottola is the man responsible for Beyonce, Mariah Carey

and many successes on Epic and Columbia. He is the man and can literally make you a superstar or guarantee you never perform again. I just tried to tell myself, "Stay cool, stay cool," but I can be honest and admit the pressure was intense.

When we finally made it into the room, it was packed with a dozen SONY execs that I probably will never see again. There was nothing particularly young or hip about them; they were very stern and unsmiling. The four of us looked at each other: This was a tough crowd we were going before, but we were ready.

We prayed right before we hit the stage. Then it was "B2K—all of the way!" We came out smoking. The first song, "Here We Go Again" (eventually it ended up on our first album), was going great. The execs seemed to be into it. We were singing like our very lives depended on it. Maybe they did. We hit all of our cues, and we sang all of the right notes—just like we had done in rehearsals a hundred times before. At one point I glanced over and saw the guys working our performance like masters. Confident, cool and in control. That moment is frozen in my mind. I was so proud of us. Win, lose or draw, right then and there, we were rocking it. We got polite applause at the windup of that first song. But before we could even get the second song started, Tommy Mottola stood up and said, "All right. That's it. I've heard enough." We didn't know how to react, but we pretty much thought that we had screwed up somehow.

They sent us out into the hall like we were being punished. After what seemed like forever, Chris and Taz came out and said, "They want to do the deal." The funny thing was that this is exactly what we had been waiting to hear, but nobody really got excited then. It was like, "That's cool." We were holding our breath for the next two days, praying that something unexpected wouldn't come along and screw up the deal. It wasn't until we got back to L.A. and we went to our attorney's office that things changed up. As soon as we signed the papers, we could feel it hit us. This thing was real now. It was really happening. Everything we had worked hard for was starting to pay off. I can't describe how happy I was at that moment. B2K was on the playing field. I called my mom and told her the good news only after the contracts had been signed.

That summer we got our first real break—a supporting spot on the Lil' Bow Wow tour—after Jermaine Dupri and the group Jagged Edge saw us perform. They had no idea who we were, but they liked what they saw, and Jermaine told Chris that Lil' Bow Wow was getting ready to tour and they needed an opener. Chris figured that this could give us some needed audience exposure while we were shopping up a record label. After all the months of rehearsal, we felt that we were ready to take the next step, and the Bow Wow tour was just that.

The first night of the tour, when we were standing backstage waiting to go on, was one of the most exciting moments of my life. But as confident as we were, I could tell all four of us were feeling sick and nervous on the inside. I think I was shaking when we hit the stage and heard the audience roar, but somehow it all came together.

We did a short three- or four-song set, but every move and every note was perfect. We were grinning all over ourselves because the moves and the singing we had been working on in the lab were now being appreciated by total strangers. They were responding to us, and we were responding to them—it was like Mr. Giles all over again, except instead of one middle-aged man it was thousands of young men and women, and they were all shouting our name.

B2K didn't have any kind of product that the audiences could relate to. We didn't have much more than our name and the desire to break through into the big time. We found out that even though we didn't have any material on the radio yet, we were really embraced by the fans. That tour was one of the best times we had. We were so happy to just take what we had been perfecting in our lab and share it with the world. The audiences appreciated it. It was a humbling experience to be embraced not for your current hit (which we didn't have) but purely for your talent. To see fans at the arenas carrying B2K signs was really special. Somebody must've liked us, because the word got around pretty fast. The signs were out there in each new venue we played. B2K was on tour and enjoying it. This was early on—we were carrying our own bags and everything. That was OK with us because we were finally out of the lab and on the road.

During that tour we developed a good relationship with Bow Wow and his entire crew, so when the tour ended they invited us to be in his "Ghetto Girls" video, and we jumped at the chance. It was our first music video, and we were real excited to be in it. The lights, camera and film crews are always exciting to be around. Of course it wasn't our video; we were just singing in the chorus and dancing, but when the video wrapped, Fizz said that this was soon going to be the way that we would be rolling, and we all had to agree with him. He was pumped. So were the rest of us. To this day we are still real tight with Bow Wow. Whenever I go to Atlanta, I never have to stay in a hotel. I can always hang with him and his mom and the rest of the crew. They are real good people.

Now that we had our deal, we had to go about the hard stuff—cutting some kicking records. Now that we had a deal, we expected we would have access to the talents and songwriting abilities of some of the industry's hardest-hitting producers. Eventually we would get to work with heavyweights like "Tricky" Stewart, Jermaine Dupri (J.D.), P.Diddy, R.Kelly, Tony Scott, J Classic and Adonis. But at the time we were still trying to find our musical voice. We were confident that we could sing anything and everything, but we needed to find material that could be uniquely ours. Dave McPherson, the

head of the Urban Division of SONY, was giving us all of these tunes that we didn't really like. They were like Backstreet Boys rejects, and we weren't really feeling any of them. For one thing, at 98 beats per minutes they were way too fast for our style. The only one that came close to sounding like what we're all about was an early version of "Uh Huh." The first recording sessions were different for us because it was the first time that we had done a session without Chris Stokes at the control board. We were used to his voice booming through our earphones.

A little later we decided to change up studios and do some recording in The Red Zone in Atlanta. By the time we got there, we were beginning to feel the session and the songs—especially "Uh Huh." Jermaine Dupri had gone in, made some adjustments and put his slam on it. The mix was sounding pretty good at last. Everybody agreed. The track was smoking.

A lot of times, for sound engineering reasons, we would each have to record our parts separately. I always liked it better when the four of us could be in the booth at the same time. The tracks were always prerecorded, but I really zoned in when we were all there together laying down the vocals. It was close to live performance, and I felt that it was more from the heart and less about mechanics. We fed off of each other's energy just like we did when we were on stage. The other guys liked recording that way too.

After a few weeks we had "Uh Huh" polished up and ready for the world. Epic decided to put it out as a single and let it do the work, as opposed to putting out a whole album of material. This was kind of a throwback to how they used to do it back

FAVORITE FOOD

Onion rings!

I JUST TRIED TO TELL MYSELF, "STAY COOL, STAY COOL," BUT I CAN BE HONEST AND ADMIT THE PRESSURE WAS INTENSE.

in Motown's day—start off with hit singles. That arrangement was fine with us. We were happy just to have a product that we were really proud of hitting the charts.

The craziest part of all this was that I was squeezing all of this activity around home and the upcoming school year. Things were so crazy that I felt that I was existing on like a thirty-hour day. I was always busy—rehearsing, recording, planning for my senior year in high school, photo shoots—everything. So much was happening I hardly had any time to chill with my family. People I knew in the neighborhood knew that I sang with a group, but they really didn't know about signing up with Epic or the upcoming

single. I kept most of that to myself until things broke big. I was like seventeen and too busy to have a steady girlfriend. That was okay, though. There would be plenty of time for all of that later. Right now I was focused on doing everything I could do to ensure that our single hit big.

A few weeks before the record dropped, we shot our first B2K video—"Uh Huh"—and it was a great introduction to the visual side of being a recording artist. We had appeared in Bow Wow's "Ghetto Girls" and were used to being on a film set, but we weren't prepared for the level of attention that they lavished on us. The star treatment was completely new to us, but it felt good right away—in fact the whole success thing was starting to feel

pretty OK. All four of us were thinking, "Yeah. I could live with this."

The production company took good care of us, and we did some serious work both days of the shoot. Lights, camera, action—and us. It was all good.

The clip was directed by Erik White, and he chose to showcase the B2K performance in several different, colorful environments. I especially like his camera work and the way he used color in the clip. He was able to capture what we felt B2K was all about. The speed. The movement. The group personality. The attitude. He got it all. He captured our identity on film.

One of the performance environments for the "Uh Huh" video was a fire set. There were these fire jets that had been built into the foreground and background of the set. There was a space in between where we could stand and sing. It was all controlled and safe. It wasn't even hot in there. Fizz started riffing on the similarities and differences between the fire set and the actual entrance to hell. It was stupid, but we kept laughing about it for the rest of the day. Fizz could always make us laugh.

The one-word description for us at that time was pumped. Every day on the countdown to our first single dropping felt like the most amazing day of our lives. The excitement was building moment by moment. The publicity was going out, and the record label was working it, letting all the fans know that something hot was about to drop. We just couldn't wait for the eleventh of the month to get here. Everyone felt that the single was going to be a smash, and we were mapping out our future plans accordingly. A mini-tour. Record store appearances. Television guest shots. Autograph sessions. This brand-new world was opening up to us, and we could hardly wait.

B2K went to New York to do some last-minute publicity for the single. A few stations had gotten an advance copy and were starting to play it. In just a couple of days the record was going to be released nationwide. We flew back from New York on the tenth. "Uh Huh" was coming out officially the next morning. On the flight to L.A., we made a plan to meet at the Colfax House the next day and check out the positive sales reports as they came in. The next day was going to be something special. We could all feel it.

The next morning, September 11, 2001 (9/11), we watched with America as the twin towers came down.

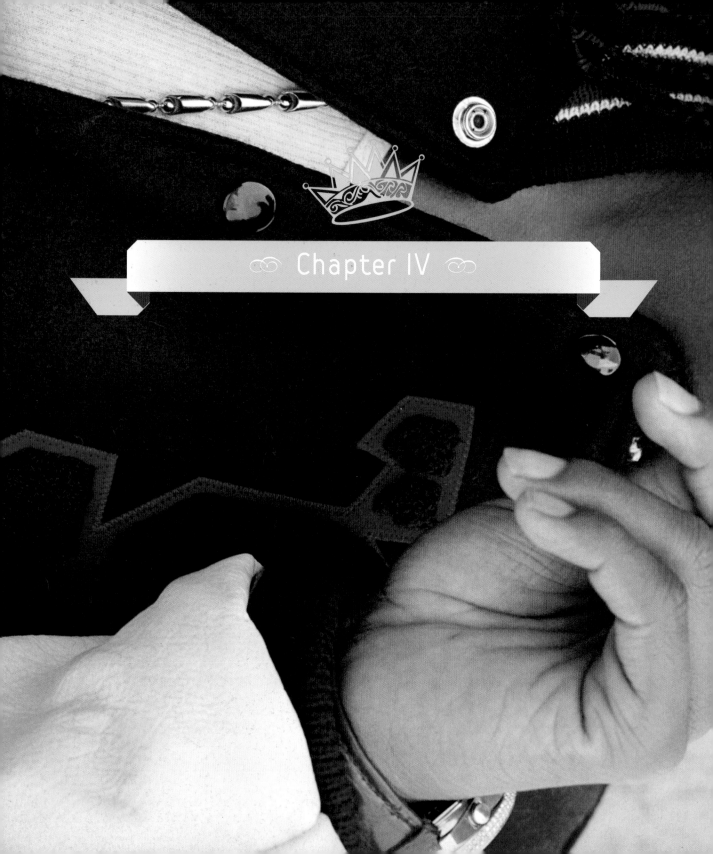

Chapter IV

BLAZIN'**UP**THE**CHARTS**

THERE WAS SO MUCH GOING ON IN THE WORLD.

WE WERE ALL GEARED UP FOR OUR SINGLE TO DROP ON TUESDAY, SEPTEMBER 11. Epic Records, T.U.G. (The Ultimate Group, our management company), family, friends and everybody else was expecting "Uh Huh" to do well. We could all feel that we had a promising hit on our hands.

And then the towers went down on that morning. We got up early so that we could start tracking the sales numbers as they came in from the East Coast. Instead we saw scenes on television that horrified us and the rest of the country. The United States had been attacked, and all we could do was watch it on television.

It was horrible. As excited as we had all been the night before, now, suddenly, nobody gave a damn about our single coming out. Not even us. B.E.T. (Black Entertainment Television) premiered our video, and it got like zero reaction. Nobody was in the audience. Nobody was paying attention. Nobody called. Nobody cared. Who can blame them? How could it be any other way? There was so much going on in the world that no one could really sit and look at a video, appreciate it and say, "Hey, that's pretty good. What's the name of that group?" That wasn't going to happen. At least not yet. The twin towers and the Pentagon were all that was on everybody's mind.

The strange thing is that we were supposed to leave New York on that morning—the morning of the eleventh. We really wanted to be home when the record dropped, and we were able to book a flight out on the night of the tenth. We went to sleep, and the next morning—there it was. It was so thick you couldn't escape it if you wanted to. As I watched the TV, I kept on saying, "We were just there! We were just there!" I looked at the television and tried to understand the pure hatred that it must take to be able to drive a plane into a building and

kill thousands of strangers and yourself. And for what? I tried to understand that kind of blind hate, but I just couldn't. I even tried to process it through my experiences with the Under Age Criminals. If you really bend the logic, you can draw some kind of a parallel between a street gangsta's life and that of a terrorist. But you really have to do some bending. The closest thing I can figure out is the selfish motive that makes you hold your ideas and your thoughts to be more valuable than anyone else's. If you think like that, then you can justify jacking somebody on a street corner or slinging crack and think it's all right. Or, thinking that same way, you can rationalize commandeering a plane and driving it into an office building. Your point of view is worth somebody else's life. That's so screwed up it doesn't even register. That's as far as my thinking would take me. I didn't want to understand or build any kind of identification with the 9/11 murderers in any way, shape or form.

For the next few weeks the country's mind was locked on the 9/11 attacks. Epic Records knew that they had hit a wall with the initial release date of our single. They recovered quickly. At the end of September they put out a twelve-inch vinyl on "Uh Huh." It actually took about six months of steady pushing for that song to catch on. It was after Christmas before it started picking up momentum. The radio stations were starting to notice us, where they had overlooked us just a few months earlier. It seemed like the single "Uh Huh" had a life of its own. It didn't want to take no for an answer. The first time that I heard it over the radio—sometime around Christmas—I pulled my car over to the side of the street and just listened. I was one happy dude. I had heard this thing like hundreds of times

while we were recording and mixing it, but it still sounded special to hear it on the air. I was so pumped that my hands trembled as I dialed up a cell phone conference call with Raz, Fizz and Jarell. We all tuned our radios to the station and just listened in silence.

Promoting "Uh Huh" was a trip and a lot of hard work. We were in and out of town so much that I couldn't keep track: it was like we were chasing the record across the country and could never quite catch up. The whole time we were hardly ever home, and it was our first experience of spending extended time on the road. We were traveling light in those days, with just a road manager and one security guy, and we weren't exactly going in luxury, unless you think a Ford Econoline is hot stuff. We were gone so much that we all got a little homesick. We were missing birthdays, holidays, all kinds of stuff.

We were in and out of radio stations all the time. It seemed like anything you could think of, some station was going to try to get us to do. To help push the record, we ended up doing all kinds of promotional stunts. A couple of ribbon cuttings, a few free midday concerts, some private parties. There was even a station down South that tried to get us to hang out in their lot and sell some cars.

A lot of stations had us come in and do contests. Most of the time the contest winners would get free tickets to our show, if we were having one. Runners-up would get CDs and T-shirts. We would sign autographs and take pictures, and sometimes they would give us gifts. There was a station in the Midwest that gave a contest where the winners got to kiss us. The station made a big production out of it. We didn't know what was going on until we got

there. The station manager had us sit at this long table while the girls were sent down one at a time. Everything went OK with Raz and Fizz; they got polite little kisses—you know, little lip smacks. However, Jarell's girl kissed him so hard that she fainted at his feet, and security had to revive her. Now this event was starting to get kind of rowdy. It was funny too. Then it was my turn. When they pulled the curtain back, I was speechless. My girl was in her midtwenties and like 250 pounds. Easily. Most of it pure muscle. The other guys and the station people were laughing their asses off. This had to be a setup, but before I could say anything, she was on me. It started out as a polite little kiss. Then she went for it and grabbed me in a bear hug. Then she was kissing me hard the whole time. I couldn't move. With a mile of her tongue down my throat I was starting to suffocate. I was struggling to get out. Then she started moaning. My guys start laughing harder. She was squeezing the breath out of me. I was starting to freak. I waved when I couldn't take any more and it was obvious that she wasn't going to let go. Security kind of pried us apart. She fell back in a chair, still moaning. I fell back on the table out of breath. Raz, Fizz and Jarell were on the floor, they were laughing so hard. Later on—after I caught my breath—I had to laugh at it too.

During this whole time out on the road in support of "Uh Huh" we became tighter and tighter with each other.

All four of us were on the same wavelength; we went everywhere together. We liked the same things and laughed at the same jokes. We were fin-

ALL FOUR PERSONALITIES WERE ABLE TO
COME TOGETHER TO MAKE B2K HAPPEN.
NO MATTER WHO STOOD OUR FRONT,
IT STILL TOOK ALL OF US TO GET THERE.

ishing each other's sentences. Even when there was some disagreement—with four strong personalities that was bound to happen—it wouldn't last long. We were having too much fun to stay mad for long. I liked the way that we were rolling. Our farts even started smelling the same. That's close.

B2K started being described in magazine articles as "heartthrobs." We all thought that was funny. I didn't see a heartthrob when I looked in the mirror, but the image was working for us, so we kicked things in that direction. We worked out a lot and stayed in shape. We always wanted to look neat and clean in our photo shoots and videos. We made wardrobe choices that reflected the "heartthrob" image. We were throwing out the young, hip, sexy vibe, and it was working. People were responding.

We all had our distinct personalities within B2K. Fizz was the joker of the group; he could find something humorous about most situations. Raz was more like the businessman of the crew. He would check out and double-check every piece of legal paper that came our way. J-Boog was more like a peacemaker. He would resolve most of the conflicts between us. He was also like our unofficial spokesperson for the group. We all had a lot to say. He just had more. I was B2K's lead singer. Not the leader of the group—the lead singer. That's an important difference, and it's how I always thought of myself in relation to the other guys.

All four personalities were able to come together to make B2K happen. No matter who stood our front, it still took all of us to get there. I respect everybody for rising to the task. A lot of people had invested their time and effort and money and were depending on us to make it. We weren't hardly going to let them down.

When we came on the scene there wasn't any kind of black boy dance group out there. There was plenty of rap going on, but not really much straight singing. We have been favorably compared to groups like New Edition, Bel Biv Devoe and Jagged Edge, and like them I think we were the right group at the right time. We had the right look, the right mix of personalities, the right moves, the right sound and the right moment. Even before we hit, we felt we were ready for the world. We were in that mind-set. We were well groomed. We were well prepared and had had a lot of artistic input from people who had the right experience and had our best interest at heart. We were ready. We were planning on being together for the long run. This was not going to be a "one hit wonder" unit. This team was going to grow old together. We knew the pitfalls, and we knew how to handle stardom. At least we thought we did. Sometimes reality has other plans.

We really didn't start to feel "Uh Huh" until after Christmas, but during the holidays we started to hear it on the radio big-time. As soon as the weather broke back east, we were gonna go on tour, and right after New Year's we started getting ready for it. Now that we had a possible big hit building, our attitude toward being on the road changed. We were not going to get homesick this time around, that's for sure.

I guess that all of the chasing and promoting was worth it, because "Uh Huh" went number one on the urban charts. Now that's something to be proud of. We were on top of the world and loving every moment of the experience.

On the road our days were full. We would usually start around five in the morning and end late, very late at night. It wasn't just a question of the show:

#1   Teen Titans
#2   Dragon Ball Z
#3   Family Matters (Steve Urkel still rules!)
#4   The Martin Lawrence Show (all-time favorite!)
#5   NFL Monday Night Football

B2K was constantly on the go—we gave interviews, visited radio stations, dropped by malls. Anything that would announce to fans that B2K was here. We quickly discovered the secret of touring: naps. Any time between interviews, appearances and shows was a good time to take a nap. "How long till the next thing?" If the answer was twenty minutes or more, it was nap time. We'd hit the floor, tables, the limo—anywhere that we could find a peaceful place for a few minutes' rest. I could swear that I saw Jarrell sleeping standing up a couple of times. But it worked out fine for us. The short naps were like power naps. They gave us the power and energy to keep rolling. Twenty minutes down, and we'd be ready to roll for another few hours.

The only thing bad about our schedule was that some of the radio people would always want us to sing in the morning. You know, something improvised on the air. Singing in the A.M. is harder than singing later in the day. Your vocal cords aren't warmed up, and your voice always sounds kinda raspy compared to the evening. We didn't particularly like to do it, but we tried to have our voices warmed up and ready. A couple of times they caught us cold. We sang, but we weren't really sounding that hot. It was kind of embarrassing. After that we started carrying herb tea and throat lozenges with us just in case.

On our first headlining B2K tour, we had a teacher on the road with us, because we were all still in high school. Not only did we have to do the performances and the promotional appearances but we also had to fit in time to go to school. And it wasn't easy, either. I remember us sitting up during the day and writing papers while we kept falling asleep. I fell asleep taking a test and woke up to find my handwriting slipping off into a sloppy line that went off the page. It was tough. The classes weren't easy. But, I tell you, school out on the road to my mind was better than regular classes. After all, we were out there and living our dreams. The school thing wasn't a problem. It was just part of the process.

Our first album dropped on March 12, 2002. Within weeks we hit the top ten on the Billboard Hot 100 chart. By that time, the album—cleverly titled *B2K*—had gone gold. Five hundred thousand units sold, and it was creeping up on platinum. Epic released a seven-inch vinyl of "Uh Huh" in April. That meant the song was crossing over from urban to pop radio. A crossover hit is a good thing. Especially your first time out of the box. It was very encouraging to know this. Nobody had given up on the record, and now it was paying off. We all believed in it.

To kick off the album, we did a promotional tour of New York City. We did a series of mini-shows, which were like a cross between a full performance and a promotional event. In one day we did a show in every borough in New York: Brooklyn,

Queens, the Bronx, Staten Island, Manhattan. Every show was packed. At every show they sold out all the CDs they had. At the end of the day we were worn out, but we were really pumped. It was like watching your talent and your audience expanding right before your eyes.

By the summer, we were really feeling good. People were treating us differently; we were getting star treatment. We were rolling like rock stars roll. All around town, fans were wearing shirts and hats with our pictures on them. We would be recognized on the streets and swarmed by screaming fans. It didn't even occur to us to carry our own bags anymore. We got all kinds of free gear, and we had a whole support crew on the road with us. There was an entire lighting crew with their own fleet of trucks, and the sound engineers had their own vans. The stagehands and roadies who built the stages at every location carried their equipment inside three big eighteen-wheelers. We had wardrobe people and a hair and makeup team. There were a lot of very interesting people along for the ride. Each group of people had distinct personalities. The wardrobe and hair people were all fly. Very fashion conscious. The roadies were mostly quiet, wore jeans all of the time and liked to climb up on things. The sound guys chuckled a lot at jokes that only they could understand. It was like a small community traveling around with you. We got our own personalized tour bus to take us from town to town. The coolest part of it was that all these people were there because of us. It felt like were leading a convoy of very cool people across the country. Hard rolling and good times. Everybody could taste a winner.

We even had bodyguards and security briefings. Those brothers were fun, yet they took their jobs seriously. For a while I resisted relying on the security people. I was used to taking care of myself, and I didn't see the need for any kind of bodyguard. I'm like, "I don't need this. I can handle whatever comes up." I soon learned that I couldn't.

One day I decided to pick up something from a store a few blocks away from the arena we were playing. It was just a quick run to the mall, so I didn't even think about security. I got down there and picked up my item with no problem. It was a nice day, so I took my time getting back to the arena, just thinking and singing to myself. I was enjoying the day so much that I didn't even notice when a couple of girls recognized and fell in beside me. They were nice kids, and we talked and joked as we walked. Some other people saw us walking and joined us. In a couple of minutes I had like twenty people walking with me. Now I was like leading a parade down the street.

Everybody was excited and talking at once. I was being friendly and cool, even stopping to take pictures and autograph some B2K shirts. I was handling the situation, but things were getting harder as more people joined the parade. I was still a few blocks away from the arena, and forward progress had been stopped. I was getting swamped, when out of nowhere one of our security guys stepped in. He told them I had to get ready for the show and to please excuse us. He was firm and gracious at the same time. The fans respected his wishes—and his size—and waved good-bye. My security guy had gotten worried about me, and I was glad he found me. The situation that day wasn't dangerous, but it pointed out to me why security was necessary. Anything can happen.

B2K was now making videos with some of the top people in the business. We were getting the video budgets to hire the best cameramen, designers and directors. Chris Meyers, Erik White and Chris Stokes were A-list music video directors. Their expertise and vision helped define our image. "Girlfriend," "Gots Ta Be," "Uh Huh," "Bump, Bump, Bump," "Why I Love You" and "Badaboom" were all good videos that enjoyed heavy rotation on all of the major music video channels. Making each one was fun, and we enjoyed doing them. Each one was like a unique, important delivery system for putting our image and music out there before the public.

The true test of our stardom was when we got onstage, because that's when you really find out if you can command an audience's emotions by making a slick move or hitting the right note: When you hear them scream, you know that you are there. And we were there. Night after night. Day after day. We enjoyed the applause. We loved the screams. We really loved giving it up for the fans. I always felt that we were in this thing together—the audience and the performer. We were both there to share something. My job was to bring some truth to the performance and to be the best that I could be. I know that a record company's "hot machine"—the promotions/publicity team—can put you out there and prop you up for a while. But the bottom line is if the audience and the record-buying public don't like you, no amount of promotion is going to make you happen. That was on us. We delivered.

It was in our blood.

The fans, especially the girls, were getting more and more intense with every show. One night, during the winter months of the Scream Tour II, we were leaving a large venue. We had just finished a meet and greet right after the show, and that meant that a lot of fans were still congregating around the entrance like an hour after the show. We came outside, and we could hear them chanting our name over and over again. Our tour bus couldn't park on the ramp because of the ice and snow that was still on the ground. As we walked up the ramp toward the bus, the shouts and chants got louder. Even though it was freezing cold, there were hundreds of our fans waiting for us when we got to the top. It was cold, and they were really going wild up there. We came into view, and they went nuts. There were barricades erected up there, but the crowd charged, and the police were having a hard time holding them back. People were surging and grabbing, and I got knocked to the ground. It seemed like something strange had happened—like some kind of invisible ray or signal had gone through the crowd. Suddenly our fans had turned into a mob. The crowd was so thick and wild that the security guys with Raz and J-Boog pushed them to the ground behind me. We had to literally crawl on the ground toward the bus. Fizz tried to stay on his feet. A woman reached over from the crowd and grabbed at him. She managed to latch onto the chain around his neck and pulled. The crowd snatched him, and I saw Fizz going up over the crowd. He was airborne. People—people who loved him—were pulling at him and hurting him. I thought he was going to get seriously injured. Raz, Fizz and me tried to get back to him, but the security guys kept pushing us forward to the bus. Chris was behind Fizz and reached up and caught him by his feet and pulled him back. They hit the ground and crawled the rest of the way to the bus. We stumbled aboard and sank into our seats. We couldn't believe what had just happened. That had been seriously scary. We could've been ripped

AS YOU MARCH OFF TO GREATNESS, TAKE THE TIME TO ENJOY THE SMALL, WONDERFUL MOMENTS.

apart if the crowd had gotten hold of us. Fizz almost was. When the bus pulled out of the lot, we looked out of the windows and saw some fans running after us, banging on the sides of the bus. It was a very weird and scary moment; we love our fans, but our clothes tear and our bones break just like everybody else's. Fans expressing themselves is one thing. Fans turning into a mob is something else. One more experience in the adventure.

At the time, B2K was always of one accord. As a group we got closer on a real spiritual level. We prayed together before every show. We should have prayed together more. All of us knew that God played the major role in what was happening. I know we all appreciated that. At least back then.

During the summer of July 2002, *The Remixes Volume 1* came out. The highlight of that summer was the B.E.T. Awards. We got the chance to perform in front of our peers, and that was really special. We did the dress rehearsal and felt that even though we were pretty tight, we could get even tighter. We went back to our dressing room and worked on our routine all the way up until it was time for us to go on. We killed it. I mean, we got a standing ovation, so it must've worked. This was a standing O from an audience of our peers. This was the upper echelon of black entertainers and performers who were standing up for us. This was really, really a great evening for us.

About this time we got our first big checks. There's something special about getting your first big fat check. It's hard not to keep looking at it and counting the zeroes over and over.

So what happens when you get that check? You go shopping—everybody does. There's no exception to that rule. I don't care how financially responsible you think you are—when that big old Russell Simmons check hits your bank account, you're gonna be in the stores. Big time. We bought clothes. We got jewelry. We bought cars. We were having a good time. Boog got a Mercedes SL500. Raz got a CLK500. Fiz got a convertible M3 BMW. I got a Benz CL600. I've got to admit that for a minute there we were like kids in a candy store.

I think all women are attractive in one way or another. If I had to be pinned down for the features that immediately turn me on, they would be:

#1: Good teeth and a great smile.
#2: A sense of humor to go with that great smile.
#3: A great body to go with that sense of humor and that great smile.

Who wouldn't be? It was fun spending that cash. We sure as hell had worked hard for it. Might as well enjoy it.

When we made it to New York again, we went to see our man—Jacob the jeweler, in the Diamond District. Jacob proudly calls himself the King of Bling. He felt it was his earthly duty to hook the music community up with some serious iced-out watches, chains and other items. One day a guy from MTV tagged along with us over to Jake's. We were in town to do a show at Jones Beach. The whole day we had been running from station to station—WBLS, Hot 97 and Kiss. We did them all. After all of that hand shaking and autographing, we couldn't wait to get to Jake's. That was our reward to ourselves. Other than the show, this was going to be the high point of the day. Jacob buzzed us in and welcomed us warmly. His place is like a velvet-and-glass trap. I've heard it said that nobody can leave Jacob the jeweler's spot without buying something. He knew our names, and he knew our music. The man obviously does his homework. He had some items already picked out for us when we got there.

Jacob showed us a special watch. The face, the hands and the numbers were all diamonds. It was like you had to shield your eyes to look at this thing. It was so bright. Jacob says, "You like that one, don't you? You want this."

He sounded like he was trying to hypnotize us. I tried this thing on, and it was like a brick attached to my wrist.

The MTV guy checked the watch out. He said, "How can you tell time with a watch like that?" I replied, "If you had this watch, you wouldn't need to tell time. Time would probably stand still for the person who owned this watch." We all cracked up. We all got something. Nobody picked up that watch, though. It was too much for even us. As we were leaving, I could've sworn I heard it calling me from the case. "Come back. You want me. Buy me. Buy me."

I think the best thing that I was able to do money-wise was to buy my mom a nice house in a nice, safe neighborhood. It made me feel good to be able to do that for her, after all of the struggling and sacrificing she did for us kids. My mom loves her house, and so do her sisters and my Nana. It's like their headquarters. Just to see them smile when they are there is worth every penny. Her favorite room is on the second floor. She has a big, comfortable chair near the window that faces out onto her favorite view, her twin apple trees. She reads, listens to music and sometimes just chills there looking out of the window. I hear from her or she hears from me at least once a day. She's always encouraging me.

In November, "Bump, Bump, Bump" dropped and

became an immediate hit. Bad Boy Records mogul P.Diddy (Puffy, Sean Combs) produced it, and I have to say, the man knows how to make a hit; he's got that magic touch. We didn't actually get a chance to work with him in the studio. We came in and just laid our tracks down separately. We did work with him on the video, though. That was an awesome learning experience just watching him work. P.Diddy is a true professional. He had every move, gesture and facial expression down to a science. "Bump, Bump, Bump" was getting massive airplay. The hits just kept on coming.

Around that same time we signed on to play the mid-1960s model of the Temptations in the network show *American Beauty*. There are five guys in the Temptations and four of us, so Marques played the part of David Ruffin. He sang the lead on the classic "My Girl," which was the song we were going to do. The Tempts are our heroes, and we felt it was an honor to be asked to do them. We studied some old footage of the original Temptations doing that song, and we nailed down their routine. For the period that we were shooting the show, we *were* the Temptations, and I think we pulled it off. When I finally saw the show, I was kind of ticked out, because the producers had insisted that I shave off my facial hair. I did, and then when the thing aired, we were in it for less than a minute. We were all over their network promos, though, as "Must See TV" for that week.

Things kept heating up. Dr Pepper wanted to do a commercial with us and the living legend Smokey Robinson.

As soon as we heard that he was doing the commercial, we jumped at it. "Smokey's in it? We're there!" In my eyes, Smokey is a true music legend. He was there at the beginning of Motown. That's almost like back at the dawning of rock 'n' roll. The commercial called for us to enter a recording studio and be surprised to see Smokey Robinson there at the mic. We join in and are honored to be there recording with him. Somewhere along the line we would drink some Dr Pepper. And that's the way it actually went down. He was a true gentleman, and it was an honor to work with him. Between camera setups, he would play the piano and tell us stories about how it used to be in the old days. He worked with Rick James, Marvin Gaye, Stevie Wonder, the Temptations, the Supremes—all legends like him. He was like music royalty. A few times during the day we joined him and got some serious harmony going. He told us he was a big fan of ours and that we reminded him of the best of the best. That for me was real special.

Smokey told us that once he was shooting a music video with the legendary Rick James out on the Pacific coast in 1984. That's the year I was born! The video was "Ebony Eyes." While the crew was shooting a scene with Rick James, Smokey took a break and came out of his trailer. He grabbed a chair and took it to the edge of the cliff they were shooting on. He sat there by himself and watched the sun go down into the Pacific Ocean. Sunset over the Pacific can be a beautiful thing. He said that that was something he hadn't done in years—watch the sun set. He had been too busy. That moment reminded him that he should take the time every now and then to appreciate the small, beautiful things in life. I guess that was the moral of the story, to enjoy what you've got while you've got it. As you march off to greatness, take the time to enjoy the small, wonderful moments. It sounded like good advice to me.

With "Bump, Bump, Bump" pounding the charts, we hit the road again. The shows were selling out. Our fan base was growing larger and larger every day. Our official website would get like a million hits a day. B2K was keeping the hits and the good times coming. We were on top of the world, and nothing was going to stop us from going as far as we could take it. Around that time we started to hear about a movie that was being built around us. Movies seemed like the next logical step for us. Bring it on. We were ready.

Chapter V

A DAY IN THE LIFE

EVERY ONE WAS SPECIAL.

A TYPICAL DAY? There never was anything like a typical day for us; every moment was fresh and exciting. When B2K was on tour, we had a routine that we tried to follow. Of course it never worked out that way. You do a lot of improvising on the road. We'd roll into town—usually by bus, sometimes by plane—and immediately set up headquarters at either the venue or at a hotel, depending on how long we were scheduled to stay. From there we'd venture out to make appearances, sightsee, shop, eat or whatever the plan was. Every day was like a different adventure.

Onstage we pretty much did the same set of songs in the same order and with the same choreography. Things may have started off the same, but that's where it ended. They never got boring or typical to us. Every performance was different. Every one was special.

We were on the road, leaving Chicago behind and heading for Detroit. We were three-quarters of the way through the Scream Tour II road show, and we were rolling cross country on the B2K tour bus. This was our third big tour in two years, and we were feeling like old pros at the tour game. Our bus was

like a self-enclosed world. We had a kitchen with a microwave and a regular stove. The refrigerator was stocked with fresh fruit, water, soda, protein drinks and plenty of snacks. There were game and computer stations, DVD setups, individual stereo systems, Internet access. Plenty of space to entertain, work and chill out. We could sleep eight people easily. The whole setup was very comfortable. We had a lot of good times on that bus. Jam sessions, rap sessions, creative writing sessions. Day or night—it never got boring.

After Detroit we were scheduled to do a couple of back-to-back dates in Kansas City, Missouri, where we would probably stay in a hotel, since we'd be doing more than one night in that city. Actually, I preferred staying on the bus to staying in a hotel room. Other people are there with you on the bus. Since I don't like being alone, the bus was always fine with me. It had everything that we could possibly want onboard already.

Here is a typical daily schedule for me—just in case you're curious!

8:37 A.M. We were up late last night talking about the show and whatever else we were thinking about. I wake up on this morning and just lay in my bed. I pull back the curtain and watch the trees on the side of the highway zip by. I'm thinking that it's Saturday—or is it Friday? One effect of being on the road a lot is that sometimes the days tend to run together. After a few minutes I look around to see who else is up. Fizz and Raz are still asleep. Jarell is up already and going through a thick stack of fan mail. On this leg of the trip we're traveling with our road manager, Twila Meraz. She's at one of the front tables, planning out the logistics of getting us into and around Detroit for the publicity events and radio dates that we are scheduled to do. Twila stays on the phone a lot. What she does requires her to solve a lot of problems on the spot and deal with the last-minute changes that always pop up. You've got to be a special kind of person to do that well. She does it well.

Jarell runs across a letter, which he hands to me. It comes from a girl in Wichita, Kansas—a thirteen-year-old junior high A student. She wants to have four little boys when the time comes. She intends to name them after us—J-Boog, Lil' Fizz, Raz-B and Omarion. Not our real names but our stage names. She included her picture. She is a nice-looking young lady with glasses who reminds both of us of our little sisters. I'm sure she'll change her mind about what to name the kids when the time comes. For right now it's a nice thought, and she obviously enjoys being there. Her letter gets placed on the pile that will get an autographed group photo from us. Jarell splits the stack of fan mail in half. He gives one half to me, and now we're both reading through them. A whole bunch of people in these letters want us to sponsor their singing group (nine out of ten times it's a B2K clone) to a record deal. Lots of luck with that.

9:11 A.M. By this time Raz and Fizz are waking up. Everybody is still groggy from the night before. We had a real good show, and nobody even thought about getting into bed until after three. Nobody got much sleep. That's going to be a little rough on us, because we've got a few promotional events to do prior to the show tonight. We've been tired before. A couple of power catnaps along the way should do the trick. We'll make it happen when it counts. We'll be good by showtime. We're always good at showtime.

The four of us drift over to a table. Somebody whips up some protein smoothie drinks in the blender. The conversation picks up right where it left off last night. The main topic is the show and everything that was happening around it. We talk about everything, from how to improve certain parts of the act to what the girls in the third row were doing. A few girls got backstage and were running around looking for us. They eluded the building security for a good half hour, too. They never caught up with us, though. Sometimes I wonder what they plan on doing once they do catch up with us.

We take what we do very seriously. You can't fake this. You've got to work hard to be the best. And we do. If you are serious about what you do then you will always be looking for ways to improve yourself. After shows we sit around and critique how it went. We might be working hard here, but we're loving every minute. Life is good. The B2K express is rolling. Sometimes it feels like I'm inside a very, very nice dream. I know you have to wake up from dreams eventually, but for right now, this is it. This is the place to be.

10:00 A.M. Everybody is starting to get hungry. We all know what that means. Denny's! Our driver has been rolling with us for a while now. He knows the story and finds us a spot somewhere on the outskirts of Detroit. I don't know how it got started, but we ended up adopting Denny's as our main eating place. It became our official spot for on-the-road comfort food. It was part of how we traveled. Of course there's better food around if you look for it. But the food here is consistent, and there's always a Denny's somewhere.

The bus unloads, and we pile into Denny's. In the morning I like to go for one of their Grand Slam meals. I like to switch up on the Grand Slams, but pancakes have got to be part of the meal. The taste of pancakes takes me back to breakfast at the old house on Bronson. I like that. When we hit Denny's at night, I'm always into their burger menu.

At the table, the four of us are talking about what we're going to do when we get back to home base—Los Angeles. The tour has been good but

long. Two straight months of traveling with only a five-day layover in L.A. in the middle. Now we are moving into the final set of dates. All of us are looking forward to getting some real time off. Fizz is thinking about going to Hawaii. Nobody has any real plans set. I know what I want to do. Nothing. All I want to do is chill at my house for a couple of weeks. That would be real nice.

Toward the end of the meal, some people seem to recognize us. They start pointing at us from the other side of the room. We finish the meal quickly and exit. Most of the time we can go unrecognized. Sometimes maybe one or two people will come up and talk to us. We don't mind. They are our fans. I remember one time we walked into a Denny's after the show, and it turned out to be the hangout spot where all of the kids who went to our concert came afterwards. We ran right into a restaurant full of excited B2K fans. They went nuts. They were acting like this was part of the show. That wasn't working at all. All we wanted to do was eat and relax. Our security guy scoped it out and suggested we back out gracefully and find another place. Something a little more remote, he said. Today it isn't anything near as hectic. We finish our meal and head back to the bus. We sign a couple of autographs along the way.

11:11 A.M. We're back on the bus and closing in on Detroit. The whole bus has gotten kind of quiet. That happens every now and then. A lot of activity, music, talking, and noise one minute. The next it would get quiet and stay that way for hours. Right now everybody is into their own thing. Fizz and Jarell have headphones on and are grooving to their music. Raz is thumbing through some fan magazines. He doesn't like that picture they used of us in one. I see what he means. All of us have our mouths open and have red eyes. We look like we're insane. I was looking for the caption to read "B2K Goes Crazy on the Road" or something like that. I remember the first time I saw us in a fan magazine. I knew it was just a picture, but there was something special about having it appear in a national magazine. Early on, every time I'd look at the picture I'd feel good about myself. My mom still has a copy of that first magazine picture. She cut it out and put it in a frame, and it's still on the wall. There have been better magazine spreads, but that one was the first. It's special.

The fan magazine gets me to thinking about the first time I realized that we actually had fans. I first saw the handmade B2K signs during the Bow Wow tour. It took me a minute to get used to it. I didn't get it at first. I can remember thinking, "Is what I'm doing really all of that exciting?" But after I saw the same thing over and over again and the number of fans growing steadily, I had to answer that question with a yes. I guess it is exciting to them. That's when I promised myself that I was always going to be my best because there are fans out there who look up to me and appreciate what I do. I'm not going to disappoint them. I'm at peace with the whole fan thing now.

We're in Detroit now. I'm trying to read too, but I end up just watching the scenery pass by. Sometimes that's the best thing to do—just chill. Everybody is just chilling and resting up. We've got a lot to do once we hit.

Our managers, Chris and Taz, are going to meet us in Detroit. They went early to take care of some last-minute business. So far we've got a radio date when we get there and possibly an in-store record promotion thing. Everybody is hoping that we can get the record store gig canceled. Meeting the public up close like that can sap your energy sometimes. Right now we're all trying to conserve. We showed up at a record store once and almost caused a riot. That's not usually the case, but it happens sometimes. That time the four of us were able to chill the crowd out. There were some anxious moments, but they worked with us, and everything turned out OK. Don't get me wrong, meeting the fans up close is real cool. We like to interact with them. It's fun most of the time. The circumstances have to be under control, though.

11:50 A.M. The bus pulls into the lot of the venue. This is a big arena we're playing tonight. The driver goes around to the stage entrance and parks on the ramp leading inside. The stage, lighting and

From the moment I saw Omari, at birth, I felt that he was here to do something special. I know now that I was right. He's doing it.

I was a single mom and a teenage mom. Omari and I grew up together.

I always saw him as an entertainer. The funny thing is that I didn't have to push him in that direction. It came naturally.

I was a dancer. I was still dancing ballet when I was pregnant with him. I did a lot of dancing with him in my arms before he could walk. That might explain his dancing skills. He really started dancing on his own at three. He amazed and entertained us all. My oldest has always been a great athlete and a winner. He knows how to win.

He has never given me any real problems. The worst thing that he did was when he was nine he asked if he could have his ears pierced. I told him no, but he and his little friend went ahead and did it anyway. He managed to hide it from me for a whole day before I busted him. I made him take it out. He didn't whine. He knew he was wrong.

I tricked him into singing. He wanted to be a rapper. I told him that kid rappers don't have longevity so he should work on his singing. He practiced singing, but he never thought that he was any good at it. He was obviously wrong about that one. I told his brother, O'Ryan, the same thing. He insisted on pursuing rapping until I let him go on the road with Omari. He saw how much fun it was, and that was the end of his rapping career.

The thing that I am most proud of Omari for is that he has stayed completely grounded. He has never lost sight of who he is or where he came from. He has always been respectful and loving. He has always brought a lot of joy into our family.

I must talk to him at least two or three times a day. And I also do his hair. That's close. Just like we've always been.

BACKSTAGE THINGS ARE BUZZING. EVERYBODY SAW WHAT WE DID WITH TEN MINUTES OF PREPARATION, AND THEY ARE IMPRESSED.

support crews have already arrived and are already at work setting up for tonight's show, which is still nine hours away.

We haul our personal gear down the ramp, around a couple of underground corridors and into the dressing rooms. We're two to a room tonight. Sometimes it's four to a room. Sometimes we each get a single. It all depends.

Our manager, Chris, is back there waiting for us. He tells us that tonight's show will be another sell-out. That's always good. The four of us high-five each other. Sellout crowds still amaze me. I guess you must be doing something right if you keep selling out arena after arena. Chris has been setting up our next set of recording sessions and photo shoots for when we get a week's break back in L.A. Our road manager comes in and hands us today's itinerary fresh out of her laptop. I see that the record promotional event is outdoors at a park. If we can fit it in, we also want to go by the original Motown building on Division Street. That ought to be interesting.

We've got an hour to chill out before we have to leave for our first event. Raz is talking to Chris about some ideas he has. Jarrell stays on the phone. Me and Fizz step out into one of those long hallways and toss a football back and forth. I get a call on my cell phone. Time out on the football toss 'cuz it's my moms returning my call from yesterday. We talk for a couple of minutes and catch up. Nothing pressing. We talk several times a week. Sometimes every day. The other guys talk to their moms just as much. She wants to make sure that I can get enough tickets for our Los Angeles homecoming show. No problem.

After I hang up, we start tossing the ball around

again. Then Fizz's phone rings, and he takes the call. I go back into my dressing room and settle in with my book. Five minutes later, it's time for us to mount up. Time seems to fly when you're in the middle of a tour. Maybe that's because you are always on the move. One thing after another. There is no downtime. Physical stamina is important.

1:10 P.M. Our first stop is at radio station WJLB. We are going in to record some station ID tags. For these shuttles around town we travel in a limo. When we pull up to the station entrance, there is a small group of kids waiting for us there. We sign some autographs, take some pictures and go inside.

We are like twenty-five minutes early for the time that has been slotted for us. Everybody knows what that means. We find a conference room, and all four of us find a place to nod out. Raz is on the table. Fizz sleeps between two chairs. Me and Jarell hit the floor. Twenty minutes later Twila comes and gets us. We spring up, ready to roll. There's nothing like a good, clean power nap.

In the booth we do about fifteen live minutes with the disc jockey. There are all kinds of B2K ticket and CD giveaways happening, and we're pumping all of that. Then the phones light up. We take another fifteen minutes of calls from the radio audience. Most of the questions are aimed at all of us. Every now and then we'll get one directed to one of us specifically. That doesn't matter. Everybody ends up answering everybody else's questions anyway. "You want to know what kind of women Raz likes? I'll answer that one!" B2K has been so tight for so long that we are easily able to finish each other's sentences. And we do.

Next we do a series of thirty-second and sixty-second station ID tags. The tags go something like this:

Fizz: Hi, I'm Lil' Fizz.
Raz: I'm Raz-B.
Jarell: I'm J-Boog.
Me: I'm Omarion.
Together: "We're B2K, and we're coming at you from the dopest radio station in Michigan—WJLB."

Then we start ad-libbing for the remainder of the spot. We are getting pretty wild up there in the booth, but it is still fun. Everybody in the room is cracking up.

Our road manager indicates that we're coming up against our time, so we wrap it up and bail. On the way out, we see that the crowd has grown a little since the time we went in. We sign a few more autographs and bounce. Everybody is happy.

2:35 P.M. Our next stop is the Motown shrine. It seems like every musical artist has to make the pilgrimage to the original Motown Records building sooner or later. We wanted to go the last time that we were in town, but we ran out of time. This time we make it. The building is really kind of small, but I guess it was really jumping in its day. We don't have much time, so we take a couple of pictures. Some people recognize us, and we take a bunch of pictures with them. We're running late for our next appointment, so we pile back in the limo and head out.

3:45 P.M. The limo pulls up to a park somewhere in the middle of the city. We check out the happenings from the car. It's some kind of all-day park party. There's a stage facing about two thousand people on the grass. Our security people want to check the scene out before we get out. While they are gone, a bunch of people come up to the tinted windows and try to see who is inside. We can see them, but they can't see us.

When security returns, they suggest that we park closer to the back of the stage and go in the back way. The limo is pulled around, and when they give us the signal, we pop out and follow them to the stage. A local band wraps up its set, then we are introduced. The crowd goes wild, and the four of us bounce out on stage. The audience surges forward, and the park security has to hold them back. Everybody is screaming so loud they can hardly hear what we are saying over the mics. "Detroit, we love you!" was pretty much it.

We toss out some B2K T-shirts from the stage. The crowd keeps pushing forward, so our guys tell us that it is time to pull out. We shout some "Peace out(s)" and follow them back to the limo. By this time a crowd has grown backstage. We have to get in a tight formation behind our security people and follow them through the crowd. This is OK today; the fans are just showing us some love. One girl grabs Fizz and plants a big kiss on him. Her girlfriend snaps a picture just at the right time. We make it back to our limo safely and climb inside. Now it's back to the arena and getting ready for tonight's show.

FEMALE TURNOFFS

#1 Bad breath   #2 Bad breath   #3 Bad breath

5:24 P.M. We're back at the arena, and the excitement is building for the show. There is a layout of food and drinks backstage. We never eat too much before a show. It makes you sluggish.

We go out onstage to do our mic check. The stage is already set up. The lights are in place, and the big screens are in position. We're ready to have a show. The sound check is routine and automatic by this point in the tour. But tonight something is not connecting. We keep getting feedback through the system. Monster-size feedback. After a few minutes, the sound engineers tell us not to worry about it; they will continue working on the audio/feedback problem.

6:00 P.M. The four of us drift out into the auditorium. We sit down and start talking about anything and everything. Somehow this has become part of our preshow ritual. We're clowning and having a good time. Our energy is starting to build. I like this part of the day right before the show. Our teamwork starts falling into place right about now. We can all feel our energy starting to build. These few minutes sitting in the auditorium help us focus.

7:00 P.M. Backstage we go to our dressing rooms to get ready. Out in front, the audience is coming into the building. In a little over an hour we will be onstage. The sound crew is still trying to work out the feedback thing.

Every now and then Raz and I put on a disguise and go out into the audience just to check things out while the opening act is performing. We just like to check out the crowd up close, or maybe we just like to live dangerously. Jarell keeps warning us that we are going to get caught out there one day without any security and get torn apart by some adoring fans. We're not worried. We haven't gotten caught yet. Besides, we're fast. We think we can get away if the situation gets too crazy. Just to make sure of a quick getaway, we are carrying all our backstage access passes. All we have to do is flash them at arena security and we can get anywhere immediately. It's always worked up until now.

We both put on big hats and sunglasses. We check ourselves out in the mirror. We think we look disguised. Jarell laughs out loud. He thinks me and Raz look like me and Raz with big hats and sunglasses on.

8:40 P.M. Raz and I slip into a side entrance while the opening act, Jhene, is performing. Jhene is Fizz's cousin, and she is doing well. The crowd is into her. We drift down to the center of the arena and check everything out. For right now we are part of the audience that came to see B2K. And this crowd came to party. We have our hands in the air, and we are swaying back and forth just like everybody else. We are deeply embedded.

About ten minutes later, we are still grooving and congratulating ourselves on the fact that nobody recognizes us when I see it. I am shocked, so I blurt out, "Raz, look at her mic! Her mic!"

We always use cordless microphones. We move around so much that we have to have cordless mics. That's the only way we can pull off our chore-

RIGHT THEN AND THERE WE GET ON IT. WE GO INTO SOMETHING LIKE A B2K ACTION MODE.

ography. But up on the stage, Jhene is using a mic with a long wire attached. That is not a good sign.

Raz can't believe it either. He gets up on a chair to get a better look. What does he want to do that for? It was bad enough me yelling out his name in the middle of that crowd, but when he gets up on that chair we suddenly realize that some people recognize us. They come right after us. This girl grabs Raz and hugs him. I pull him away, and we break.

It's like an obstacle course getting out of the auditorium. We run outside into the concession area and are immediately recognized by another group of fans. They come right after us too. We run hard. I am hoping that the cops won't see us running through the arena, not recognize us and jack us up. That's all we need: to get jacked up by the cops at our own show. Right now, though, I am more scared of the crowd coming after us. We run, dodge, leap over some barricades and take a couple of wrong turns. There are two sets of fans coming at us from both sides, and we are stuck in the middle.

At the last minute we duck into the men's room. We catch our breath and dash out the other end. We flash our access badges and finally make it backstage just ahead of those people chasing us.

We are still out of breath when we make it back to the dressing rooms. Despite the bad news about the microphone situation, Fizz and Jarrell have to laugh at the fact that we almost got caught out there this time. The laughter doesn't last long: We have a crisis on our hands. The word has already gotten backstage. For some technical reason, we can't use the cordless mics tonight. We'll have to work around the wires. That's four sets of long wires to trip over. Not good. Not good at all. How are we going to pull this one off?

9:05 P.M. Right then and there we get on it. We go into something like a B2K action mode. Everybody is dead serious now. We attack the problem head-on. We go into a rehearsal room backstage and get in front of the mirrors. We can't rechoreograph the whole show, but we can work out the first song. If we can work that one out, maybe we can get into the rhythm and improvise the rest of the show. Maybe. We start working real hard. For a moment it is like we are in front of the mirrors back at the Colfax House. That seems like a long time ago. So much has gone down since then.

The whole trick is to keep the choreography moving while not getting tripped up in the wires. At first we are looking pretty crazy. I spin, Jarrell tosses me a mic and it hits me in the head. We are dropping the mics. Getting caught up in the wires. Colliding into each other. Falling down. Tripping over each other. It's a mess. We're like clowns at the circus. All that is missing are the red noses and the big shoes.

9:20 P.M. We're running a little late. The crowd out there is getting restless. The pressure is on, but I honestly think that we are all getting off on the challenge. Our energy is starting to flow off of the chain. Things start to work. The choreography, microphone wires and all, is starting to fall into place. We're all starting to feel it. Chris tells us that we're fifteen minutes past showtime. We always take pride in hitting the stage on time, every time. Ready or not, now is the time.

9:30 P.M. Right before we go onstage we huddle up and say a little prayer. Any way you look at it, this is going to be a different kind of B2K show. We can hear the crowd going crazy in anticipation just a few feet away from us. The lights go up, and we hit the stage. Everybody is pumped now—it's like we're going into battle or something.

We start singing, and then we start passing microphones off to each other. At one point I spin, put my mic on the floor and J-Boog leans down and grabs it up. Raz tosses his mic up, and Fizz grabs it out of the air. The choreography is really looking tight. We are flowing with the moment. The crowd is into us one hundred percent. They really get off on what we are doing with the mics. They think that stuff is tough—and, I've got to be truthful,

it is. It all seems like part of the act. Once we get through the first number, we have it figured out. Even when we make a mistake, we are moving so fast that nobody picks it up. We are feeling it. B2K kills that show.

Right after our encore, we run off the stage and embrace each other in this big group hug. It feels good. Chris and Taz join us in the hug. They were watching the show from the wings, and they say that we were on top of our game. We hold onto each other for a good while. If I had to pick a single best B2K performance, that would be the one. I think the others would agree.

Backstage things are buzzing. Everybody saw what we did with ten minutes of preparation, and they are impressed. A couple of the Detroit Pistons stop by with young relatives to congratulate us. We feel like we've done something special tonight.

11:25 P.M. Eventually we make our way back to the bus, which is still parked on the ramp. We are still feeling good and now a little hungry too. That can only mean one thing—Denny's! A group of fans has gathered around the entrance of the ramp. They just want to wave and tell us how much they enjoyed the show. It's all good tonight. I'm on top of the world.

12 A.M. At our favorite eating spot we finally get a chance to relax. We are still buzzing from the show. The adrenaline rush is still with us. As we're wrapping up the meal, I can see that the young waitress kind of recognizes us. Kind of—she's not sure.

As we are leaving, the waitress comes out behind us. She's kind of shy and says, "Excuse me, but are you—?" Before she finishes her question, I turn to her and start singing "Gots Ta Be." I pick up the song somewhere in the middle. Fizz, Raz, and Jarell hear what's happening and double back. They all jump in, and suddenly we're performing the song a cappella right there in the parking lot. A couple more waitresses come out, and now we have an audience of three. We're hitting our moves just like we're on the stage. When we finish, the three of them applaud like they mean it. They enjoyed it. But I think we enjoyed it more.

1:10 A.M. Back on the bus we stretch out and unwind. Tonight's show was a real great experience for everybody. One of the best. It drained us, but it was a good kind of drain. We earned it. We talk some more about the show, the rest of the tour, vacation, other people's music, what's at the movies. We talk about everything.

2:30 A.M. Eventually Fizz and Jarell drift off to sleep. I'm still a little bit wired, so I look for a DVD to put on. That should help me ease down. Most of the stuff in the stack I've seen before. Some of them I've seen several times. I think we've seen The Five Heartbeats at least fifteen times. The Matrix ten times. I find something at the bottom of the pile that I haven't seen before. It's in an unmarked case. The film is A Hard Day's Night, and it stars the Beatles. I'm not sure why, but somebody suggested that we should take a look at it. Why not? It's late. I watch about five minutes, and then rewind it to the beginning. Raz is dozing in the chair next to me. I shake him awake and point at the monitor. I start the DVD again. After the first couple of scenes, he sees what is happening. The movie opens up with a crowd of girls—big fans—chasing the Beatles down the street and into a train station. They run, jump, dodge and finally escape the crowd of fans by running onto the train.

Me and Raz just look at each other and crack up. Isn't that the exact same thing that we just went through earlier tonight, at the arena? Our escape was just like what was happening on the screen. Unbelievable.

3:14 A.M. Everyone is now in bed. Before I drift off, I run through the day one more time. The day was exciting and, as usual, action packed. We did a lot and ended up giving one of our best live performances. We were forced to think quickly and come up with a strategy. Looking back, this was a very good day and a hard day's night. I loved it. On to Kansas City.

Chapter VI

GETTING**SERVED**

Chapter VI

COME STRONG WITH THE DANCING OR DON'T COME AT ALL.

A FEW WEEKS AFTER "BUMP, BUMP, BUMP" HIT THE CHARTS, the word came down to us that the movie Chris had been trying to get off of the ground for the past couple of years was finally going to happen. The script was originally titled *Dance* and was about the whole street dancing/battle dancing thing that's hot on the L.A. underground scene.

The story is about Elgin and David, two friends who lead a street dance crew. They take on all challengers, split up, make up and get back together just in time to win the big dance-off competition. It is a simple story, but the way Chris talked it up, it was going to be hot. There were going to be pretty girls, off-the-chain dancing, bad guys being bad guys and good guys who finally win at the end. There had been other street dance movies we'd seen, like *Breakin'* back in the eighties, but the vision for this one was something special. After reading the revised script, I agreed. This could be something special. The new title was *You Got Served.* Kind of appropriate, huh?

Chris Stokes had directed like a bunch of music videos. Over fifty. He had also done a movie— *House Party 4: Down to the Last Minute*—starring the guys from IMX. He badly wanted to do another movie, and he figured that the time was right for *You Got Served.* He took the script to Clint Culpepper at Screen Gems, and they went for it. We got a quick green light. I guess he looked at all of the elements—music, dance, youth culture, B2K— and decided to take the risk.

The picture was budgeted at under ten million dollars, which isn't a lot of money by today's standards. Ten million dollars certainly doesn't seem like a little bit of money to me; I know I could invent some uses for it. What that number meant as far as the film was concerned was that there had to be an intense rehearsal and preproduction period, because once the cameras started rolling, we had to have our act together. We didn't have the money or the time to do anything else but that. And the amount of dancing that the story was built around meant that a lot of hard work was going to go down in a short period of time. We were under some serious time pressure as soon as we got the go-ahead. B2K was already committed to headlining another tour starting in late July. We had to be finished with the movie in early July in order to get in all of the rehearsal necessary. That was not a lot of time to put a good movie together. Putting any movie together— especially one with a twenty-four-day shooting schedule—is hard work. To take advantage of the time available, everything had to be planned out in detail before the cameras rolled.

But we looked at it like a big challenge. We were all ready to step off onto the next level—movies. B2K was rolling, and we were ready for it. I know that Marques and Chris were ready too.

It was perfect timing, and everything was coming together just they way we wanted it to. All that was left was for us to do our part, so we did what

we had to do and made it happen. Correction—God made it happen.

I was supposed to play the role of Rico. Rico was a supporting character and one of the crew's ace dancers. They were originally looking at Jarell to play David, the coleader of the group. Chris came to me one day and said he wanted me to play the role of David. I told him that I had already been working on the character of Rico and was comfortable playing him. He said, "Trust me. You're perfect for David."

I knew I was a strong reader, but I still had to convince myself that I could give up a good performance on the screen. Fizz and Raz came across well in the videos, but they had never acted before. Jarell was solid but had never done any work either. I had done a national cereal commercial and a McDonald's spot—I wasn't a stranger to the camera. Marques Houston was already set to play Elgin. Me and Marques have natural chemistry. We've got that older/younger brother thing happening. All four of us couldn't do the role. Only one of us could. Chris was comfortable and confident that I could deliver the role, and ultimately it was his decision—I didn't even have to read or audition for any of the studio people.

Eventually the studio went along with Chris's recommendation. I discussed it with the rest of the group, and everybody said they were cool with it. "Whatever's best for the project" was how they put it.

So now I was going to be David. I could handle that. It was a big step for me—costarring in a major motion picture—but I was going to be ready when the time came to step up. Jarrell ended up playing the part of Rico.

We were able to squeeze in a month and a half of rehearsals, most of which was spent on the dance sequences. Some of it was devoted to character stuff. Marques and I worked both sets of rehearsals. It was a lot of work, but it was cool; we had a whole team of choreographers working with us. Even Dave Scott, who we had been working with for years and who did our videos, was onboard. We also had Shane Sparks adding his expertise into the mix. Smooth and Robert Robertson helped out also. In the area of street, hip-hop and modern dancing, this was the A-Team. And we had some of the best street dancers in the nation involved with us. These were really some dynamic dancers; the talent we had on the set was off the chain. It was a very creative atmosphere to be working in. As far as I was concerned, we were going into this project strong.

The routines that the choreographers were coming up with were unbelievable. We knew that in some ways *You Got Served* was going to be compared with break dancing movies like *Breakin'* and its sequel, *Breakin' 2: Electric Boogaloo*. We wanted to make the dancing so dynamic, so tough and so fresh, that there would be no comparison with the earlier movies. We were aiming for the audience to go like, "Whoa! That's dope!" Not once—but several times.

Everybody on the creative end agreed that traditional street dancing had to be updated and would have to be shot in such a way that the audience would know right away that they were seeing something special. Along with the street dancing they were going to include elements of jazz, acrobatics, ballet, hip-hop and some fraternity step moves. Everybody was excited. Even though the choreographers were in charge of creating the actual routines, they were always open to creative input. They left it open so that the dancers felt free to bring some of their own moves and improvisations to the mix. A lot of good ideas got exchanged.

Chris Stokes decided to shoot the dancing in a different way. A lot of the new stuff you see has that MTV cut—editing dance moves so that they seem faster and flashier. You've seen it before. A close-up of feet moving, another close-up of the dancer's eyes. A quick cut of some kind of movement, more quick cuts. Sometimes things are moving so fast that you really can't see what the dancers are doing. Chris wanted to shoot it so that you could see everything that the dancers were doing. Could actually see them dancing instead of posing. He wanted to let the moves speak for themselves. A lot of the movie was shot wide enough so that you could see everything going on from head to toe. This is the way that guys like Fred Astaire and Gene Kelly used to shoot their dance numbers way back in the day.

The director of photography on the film was going to be David Hennings. The last movie he shot prior to *You Got Served* was *Blue Crush*, that surfing

movie with all of the fine girls in it. I liked the way that film looked and was glad that he was down with us. He's the one responsible for creating all of those beautiful surfing shots, so I knew he could capture the excitement we were planning on bringing to the dancing.

The whole story of battle dancing is pretty interesting. I think that we were the first movie to actually deal with it. We did some research and checked out some of the hottest crews battling each other. I was knocked out; some of the things those guys were doing seemed to defy gravity. There was some serious dancing going on. What we'd be doing in the film had to be just as good, if not better, to nail down the credibility on the street. If we showed up with some fake stuff, the movie audience was going to let us know about it. They know what's real.

Battle dancing started out basically as an alternative to conflicts. Groups challenge each other, and instead of using fists or guns, they resolve things by seeing which group can outdance the other. Crews start putting together some elaborate dance routines, and the challenge goes out. Money is put into a pot, and the winners are picked by a panel of judges or, usually, by audience reaction and applause. To win, you really have to be showing them something dope. When what you're doing is working and the audience likes it, they're going to let you know. The trick is that everybody is good. All of the dance crews have got good moves and slamming routines. For real. The success of *You Got Served* was going to depend heavily on the dancing. It all came down to that simple truth: Come strong with the dancing or don't come at all.

A demonstration was staged for the Screen Gems/SONY people a week before shooting began to show them how we were going to shoot the dancing and what the dancing was actually about. It was the first time that a lot of those executives had seen anything like it. They were impressed.

All of a sudden, preproduction was over and it was time to start putting film in the can. Day number one—the first actual shoot day—of the production schedule had come up on us real fast. The read-throughs, the dance rehearsals, the acting rehearsals, the wardrobe sessions, the location scouting and the test shootings were all over now. The doubt that you get when you are about to take a big step was starting to get to me. During production, it was easy to project self-confidence because everybody was so busy putting the movie together that they didn't have time to pay attention. When the cameras start rolling, it's another story. Sometimes it's like you're out there by yourself, and the cameras don't lie. Just you, the camera and sixty or seventy crew people paying attention to everything you do.

Right before we started shooting, I had to have a talk with myself. "Get it together, O! You've got this." I put myself in the same place I like to be in at a live performance. "This is your stage. You own this stage. Nobody can touch you while you are on this stage." It worked. The nervousness faded. I went in front of the camera and did my thing. It was all dope from that point on.

I thought that we'd probably start off shooting a simple dialogue scene. Something like a two-person conversation. Something easy and uncomplicated to shoot so that the cast and crew could get into the rhythm of the shoot. Instead of the simple dialogue scene, Chris started us off with the scene in which Li'l Saint is pronounced dead at the hospital. He wanted the first day of shooting to include all of us—B2K, Marques, and the girls.

There was some serious drama going on in that scene. Jarell as Rico finds out that his little friend, like a little brother almost, has been killed. Jarell gave it up—he punched the wall in anger, and it felt to me like that stuff was real. He made me believe it, and I was acting in the scene with him.

From that point on, I kind of felt like we were really on to something.

On day four we kicked off with a big dance scene. That was the start of a real wild time. There was a lot of great energy, and everybody hung in tough. We needed to shoot a lot of footage to make sure Chris ended up getting the shots he needed. We were shooting a lot of the dance scenes in this old carpet factory in Glendale, which turned out to be the perfect location for the dance battle competitions that Mr. Rad sponsors. We usually shot the dance sequences with three cameras, because there was so much going on. When a crew performs, you have people spinning, flipping, leaping and doing splits all at the same time, and it takes that many cameras just to get it all. Sometimes we would have to repeat a segment five or six times so that we could get it from different angles. That worked for me. The more times we did it, the better it felt—everybody's energy just got stronger with each take.

Staging and filming the dancing sequences was the high point for me because I was proud of the work that I did; I felt like I was battling big time. Everybody was really into the battles, and the funny thing is that nobody—none of the dancers—wanted to lose. Even though the script said one thing, the dancers were really trying to win like it was a real competition. A few of these guys couldn't help it. They were from real crews, and competition was what they lived for. Sometimes at the end of a take they would keep the music playing, and suddenly a real battle would break out. Some of those shots are in the film. I even managed to get a couple of unscripted moves into the mix. I did an improvised back flip, and it just happened

to work perfectly with everything else that was going on in the shot. It's in the finished film.

Mr. Rad was played by Steve Harvey, and he's even funnier when the cameras are not on. Steve really worked to make his Mr. Rad character a positive role model, and he was the same way off the set, always positive and encouraging to us. Steve would hang around to watch the dancing even when he wasn't in the scene. He just wanted to support us and see the dancing sequences coming together. He could've been in his trailer chilling or on his way home, and we appreciated him taking the time.

Steve Harvey also bought a suit for each of us in B2K; he said we had everything else, but what we really needed was suits, and he was right. He really hooked us up; we looked seriously good in those suits, too. The four of us wore them out to a club one night, and we stopped traffic. I took my mother out to dinner one night in that suit. It was a fancy place, and she just couldn't stop smiling at me and my new suit.

The female leads were played by two beautiful and talented young women—Meagan Good and Jennifer Freeman. They were great to work with, too. Meagan played Marcus's love interest, and Jennifer played Marcus's sister. Me and her hook up, and that's one of the things that my character, David, and Marcus's character, Elgin, have a dis-pute about. It was a big part of their conflict. I did my first screen kiss with her. It was so good that I wanted to do a couple of extra takes—just to make sure we got it right.

After they split up, David and Elgin have a bunch of bad run-ins. We filmed all of those scenes in the same week. During that time Marcus and me stayed away from each other. We barely spoke. It built up the tension between us, and that worked for what was happening on the screen. In the story things get so bad between the friends that Elgin ends up taking a swing at David, and in the script he connects. We rehearsed with the stunt coordinator a couple of times and decided we were ready to shoot it. Every time Marcus would throw the punch with the camera running, I'd block it. Even though David is supposed to get tagged, I kept instinctively blocking the punch. After the second take it got funny. We finally got it together and did a good take. In the film I think it looked pretty convincing.

We did a lot of shooting at the Mr. Rad space, and Chris was driving us hard. Nobody minded. We all knew what was at stake.

That carpet warehouse was so big that we were able to create entire sets in some of the other rooms. There was a lot of activity going on in that building. Man, there were so many different kinds of dancers and styles of dancing on the set. I was like a sponge soaking it all up. We had a whole

HEROES & ROLE MODELS

1. God, for setting the whole thing up
2. Martin Luther King, for being a visionary leader
3. Malcolm X, for being a visionary leader
4. Chris Stokes, for being my manager and friend

JARELL GAVE IT UP—
HE PUNCHED THE WALL IN
ANGER, AND IT FELT TO ME LIKE
THAT STUFF WAS REAL.
HE MADE ME BELIEVE IT, AND I
WAS ACTING IN THE SCENE WITH
HIM. FROM THAT POINT ON,
I KIND OF FELT LIKE WE WERE
REALLY ON TO SOMETHING.

community of dancers there every day, just grooving off of each other. There would always be these great vibe-out sessions during breaks, between camera setups and after hours. There were also several impromptu battle sessions. Hey, with that many dancers on the set, that's the only way it could be. It was a wonderful, fun experience. I learned a lot being on that set.

I've heard a lot of stories about actors and stars trippin' out. Making demands. Working everybody's nerves. None of that existed on the *You Got Served* shoot. Everybody was cool and professional. That's why I enjoyed it so much.

A reporter came to interview me on the set one day. He asked me what I enjoyed most about the filmmaking process. I told him that it was the acting. The acting and what you bring to getting ready to play a part. Building the character is what it's all about. Not everybody understands what it really takes. They think that acting is like reciting dialogue or expressing yourself in a certain way. It's really about how you deliver the character and how you make him pop; you've got to believe in the character to the point where what you do is what the character would do. The specific things he does have got to be real; you have to invent how your character reacts to things. You've got to add detail to your interpretation of the character. You know, the things that make it pop. The way he stands. The way he listens. The way he picks his nose. All of that. The lines of dialogue will come. The character building comes first. I'm still learning, but I do know this—if you're going to be a good actor, you've got to take it seriously. That doesn't mean you can't have fun with the whole thing. I'm always going to do that. But for me it means that I know that I'm going to have to treat acting as seriously as I do performing live and singing. My goal is to be an all-around entertainer. Movies and acting are a part of that.

While we were filming, "Bump, Bump, Bump" was still getting heavy airplay on the radio. The records were selling big, I was starring in a big movie—I couldn't believe how blessed I was. It was a busy time, and I loved every moment of it. Sometimes we would wrap up filming for the day and go

I REMEMBER THINKING, "HEY, MAYBE THIS COULD WORK." AFTER SEEING THE FIRST SET OF DAILIES, THE BUZZ WAS STARTING TO GET AROUND THAT WE HAD A HOT PROJECT GOING ON. ALL THAT DID WAS FIRE US UP SOME MORE.

directly to a radio date. The tour was starting up in late July, so as soon as we wrapped filming we were going to begin rehearsals for the show. It was a hard schedule, but we kept our focus, and everything worked out.

At the end of the first week of shooting, we saw some of the dailies. The dailies are all of the raw footage that is shot. No editing. No effects. Just straight-up footage. For the first time, I think, we all got an idea of what we were dealing with. We knew something was up. What was up on the screen was working. The individual shots were looking good. The dancing was like coming out of the screen at you. I remember thinking, "Hey, maybe this could work." After seeing the first set of dailies, the buzz was starting to get around that we had a hot project going on. All that did was fire us up some more.

We wrapped up shooting on time. We had put so much energy into the project that I really couldn't believe it was over. The wrap party was at the Key Club on Sunset Strip. It was a cool way to end an intense experience. Everybody had worked hard and now was there letting off steam. Two days later, rehearsals for the new B2K tour began. By now we were used to the pace, so we just kept rolling with it.

Somebody figured out that a good way to build some excitement for *You Got Served* was to show a trailer on the big screens during our concert performances. They put together a trailer real quick,

and it was scheduled to be shown at some point during the show. We looked at the schedule, and it just said "Show promo trailer here." We had no idea what it looked like or how it would go over. The first time we saw it was the first time an audience saw it. We came out from backstage and checked it out. From the very first moment, the crowd went wild. We were high-fiving each other when it was over. The word was going out. Audience awareness was happening. Every show, it was the same thing. We just might have a hit movie on our hands.

Screen Gems was testing the movie at sneak previews across the country in December. The response was very favorable, and they were seriously encouraged by the reports they were getting. The publicity department got into it, and commercials started showing up on TV. Word of mouth was all out on the street. If you were part of the youth culture, this was the movie to see. The movie was scheduled to open in January on Super Bowl weekend. I got excited the closer that date approached.

The *You Got Served* premiere was held at the Chinese Theater in Hollywood. A lot of big-time premieres are held there, and the whole affair was fly. We got the full red carpet treatment and had a slamming afterparty. I loved it.

There was only one bad thing: I didn't see the other guys at the premiere or the afterparty. By the time of the premiere, I was sensing that something

MUSICAL INFLUENCES

I like to listen to a lot of different stuff. All kinds of stuff. Hip-hop, rap, country, R&B, pop and jazz. My favorite singers are gospel recording artists like Kim Burrell, Eric Dawkins and Tonex. They can hit the mark with their emotion each time. I've even listened to Nat "King" Cole. That guy was smooth.

was up. I felt bad about that, but I wasn't going to let it spoil my moment of triumph, so I pushed my concerns to the back of my mind.

On Super Bowl weekend the movie opened across the country. In that first week we showed $16 million in ticket sales, which was huge. People really liked the movie—some were even going to see it two and three times. And we had been right—the dancing was dynamic. The critics loved the dancing and gave the drama a passing grade. That was OK, though. The movie was a hit. At the box office alone it took in like close to $50 million domestically.

I read that there were some fighting incidents at a Lakewood theater on opening night. The cops even had to arrest a bunch of people. I don't understand the problem; it certainly wasn't what was happening in the movie that was feeding the violence. The film wasn't about that kind of stuff at all. In fact there's hardly anything violent in *You Got Served.* Our movie was about youth and energy, and it crossed racial lines. If anything, it was about

settling things through nonviolent means, on the dance floor and not on the streets.

A couple of months later I was surprised to learn that I had been nominated for two MTV movie awards. One nomination was for best dance performance. The other one was for best breakout male actor. You talk about being happy—just the recognition that comes with being nominated was enough for me. It was a huge honor, and it told me loud and clear that I had an acting career now. I was in the game.

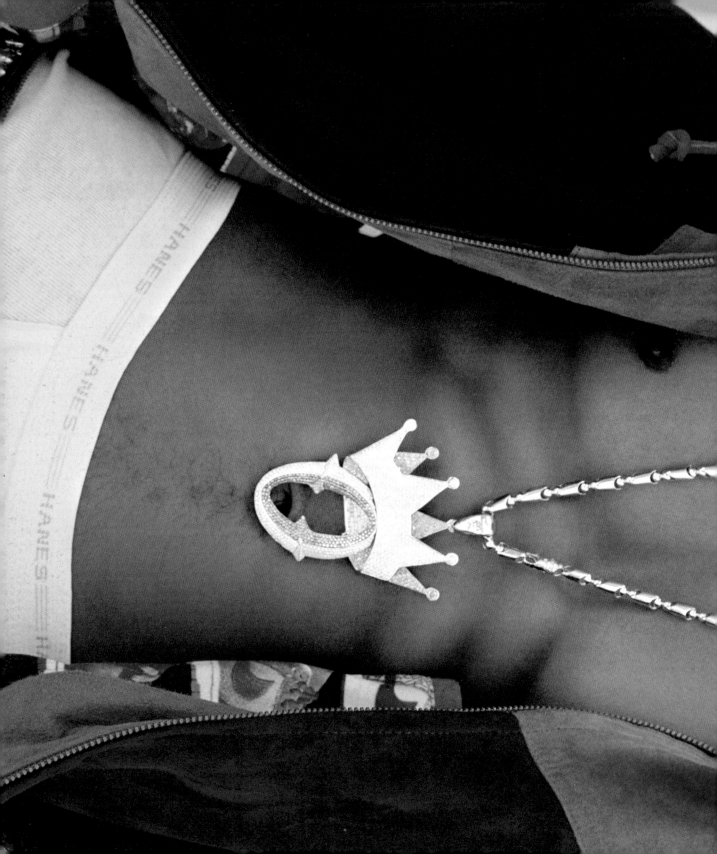

THE**FALL**OUT  Chapter VII

I GUESS I SHOULD HAVE FELT IT COMING.

ALL OF THE SIGNS WERE THERE, but I was just too busy having a great time to realize it. It was like in boxing; you see a punch coming at you but your feet are planted, you're out of position, and the blow catches you. I got caught.

My guys—Raz, Fizz and J-Boog—caught me off guard. The personal impact was worse than you could imagine. My best friends ended up sneaking me. I felt betrayed; it was like I was getting banked on the sidewalk by some strangers. The things that were being said did not sound like they were coming out of the same guys that I had spent almost every day of the last three years with. The accusations, the bad vibes, the public dissin', the final breakdown—all of that took me by surprise. Big time. I guess the signs were there, but I failed to see them. I was enjoying being a part of the B2K experience too much to notice that something wasn't right.

So, what was the problem? How did a group of talented and extremely lucky young men who had the world on a string break up? How did that happen? The short answer: It got complicated. Once egos hit the equation, it always gets complicated.

Let me just state a simple fact. We were B2K. I mean, we were one of the hottest acts in pop music. Period. I'm talking about the top of the top. Nobody could touch us. We were hitting with gold and platinum singles and albums every time out. We were selling out every stop along our concert tours. Our videos were slick. They entered the charts in heavy rotation and stayed there. Our fan base was super large, crossover and growing every day. We had it all. Pardon the language, but we were the shit.

On a personal level we were friends. These were the guys you went into battle with. We were like a band of brothers. Unimaginably tight. We knew each other's moves. Each of us knew how the other three were thinking, or so it felt. We had bonded, and I thought that's the way it was going to be. We had watched *Five Heartbeats* several times and had all agreed that that was not going to be the way that we were going out. I felt like we were going to be like the Temptations. That we were going to grow old together as a team. I guess not.

So when it hit me in the face that there were problems—major problems—I was unprepared for the fallout. I guess if you don't want to see something, you won't.

I don't want to say it was all one way—like it was all their fault and none of mine. Usually when two sides disagree, the truth is somewhere in the middle. Usually. It did line up being three against one. That was rough, because like I said, we were a tight-knit crew. We were used to doing things as a team. All of a sudden that seemed to stop. Maybe it was growing up or growing older, but there came a point in the middle of 2003 where we stopped doing things together. We kept doing the professional things—the concerts, promotions, photo shoots—but it was the other, social things that dropped off. Like going shopping or hitting one of the bling spots. We used to come in hard together. Now it wasn't working that way anymore; people seemed to want to hang less and less. We'd be invited to an A-list industry party and we'd agree to meet at a certain time at the party so we could go in together. The other guys would show up late or sometimes not at all. Some of that was understandable—people get busy, everybody has his own life to live.

When things spilled over into our business, I began to notice. I think it started with the miscommunication. Like we'd be scheduled for a rehearsal and the other guys would either be late or not show at all. Hey, that wasn't what B2K was about—not at all! We'd started off doing things in a professional manner: You make an appointment, you show up on time, do your job and that's it. That's the way we were trained. That's the way we were supposed to be carrying it. I didn't get it—a couple of times I'd

be at the rehearsals by myself, just waiting. When I finally got through to somebody on the phone, I'd get some lame excuse, like they thought it was scheduled for later that day. Or the next day. Once maybe. But not three or four times. That wasn't working. Like I'm going to waste my time waiting around when these guys are pulling this stuff? No way.

Then it was the secrets. It felt like there were all kinds of secrets being discussed and being hidden but I wasn't in on any of them. Something was going on. But what? It got so that it was obvious that there was something on everybody's mind, but nobody was saying anything. The way I feel is that if you're on a team—or in any kind of relationship, for that matter—if there's a problem, you talk it out, let me hear what you have to say man to man. Don't keep it to yourself. That's only going to make matters worse. Nothing is going to get solved that way, and nothing did.

It was a subtle shift in attitude, but I could feel it. I was starting to feel the distance widening, and I was a little concerned. I pulled each one up individually and asked what was up. They told me that everything was cool. I had to take that at face value. But in the back of my mind I could feel that things just weren't connecting the right way anymore. Up on

NOBODY KNEW IT AT THE TIME, BUT THAT ENDED UP BEING OUR LAST SHOW TOGETHER.

the stage we were still killing it. We were still selling out and still giving a good show. Our fans still loved us. But backstage things just were not as fun as they once had been. Touring and performing is always tough, but it can be fun too. Now we were going about it like a job. At the time I thought, "Hey, give it some space, some time, and things will work themselves out." After all, we were B2K. We were in it for the long haul. No bs was going to drive us apart. We had too much going on to think about it.

We had a lot to lose. We decided to finish the tour for the fans—all four of us. We were winding down on the Scream Tour III. *You Got Served* was in the can and completed. It was scheduled to hit the screens in late January. I was excited about that because I thought that the movie had a chance of being a hit. The reaction from the audience when we showed the trailer indicated to me that we might have something unique and hot on our hands. We had a few days off over the Christmas holidays, and we were going to pick things up again with the tour in late December. Shit hit the fan at an L.A. show. Things blew up, words were exchanged, and we almost came to blows. It was some personal bs. We had called it quits that night. Chris sat us down and told us we still had a few dates left in January. I was thinking that it'd be good to take some time off, and then maybe we would have a chance to fix things. Or they could heal themselves. Whatever. The time off was going to be a good thing for all of us.

Our last concert before the breakup was in Washington, D.C. December 28, 2003. Nobody knew it at the time, but that ended up being our last show together. ATL, the Rascals and O'Ryan were on the show also. We closed it out. Nobody said much in the dressing room. When we were about to go on, I remember us all hugging each other tight. That felt

like the old days, when we were first hitting the road. We held that embrace for a minute, as if it would be our last, and then we hit the stage in our Lakers jerseys. Three of us were wearing Kobe's number—#8. Nobody seemed to mind, though, because B2K was in the house. And we turned it out. We had a good performance that night, but afterwards it was kind of quiet. I remember clearly seeing Jarell take off the jersey that he'd worn onstage, tossing it onto a chair and walking away. It happened like it was in slow motion. He never went back to get the jersey, he just left it there. That night I got really sick and ended up at the hospital. They did a CAT scan and determined that I needed further testing. I was uncomfortable being out of town receiving treatment without my family here. We decided I would go home to L.A. to get checked by my doctor. I went home and everything was okay—just fatigue. I spent the next week chilling out.

It had been a busy year, and it felt good to settle down, even if it was for only a minute. One day real close to New Year's, I got a call. I was simply hanging at my crib, cooling it by myself, when one of my friends dialed up and told me to turn on the radio. "Turn to the BEAT," he said. "Now!" I tuned in and felt like I had gotten hit by a lightning bolt from out of the blue. I was taken completely by surprise when I heard the familiar voices of Fizz, Raz and J-Boog giving an exclusive interview to the DJ. They went for it—hard-core. All of the secrets that they'd held in came spilling out over the air. They talked bad about me, really bad. They talked about the attention I was getting. What? They shot down the management (Chris Stokes and The Ultimate Group) and practically called them crooks. They bitched and complained about their money, Marques Houston and everything else. I couldn't believe it. I remember saying out loud, "Are they serious? This has got to be a joke."

I was hearing some raw stuff. They were ragging hard—I mean, take-no-prisoners stuff. I got a couple more calls from people while the interview was going out live. Listening to them, I picked up that things had started slipping at the time we were making the movie. There had been a little jealousy

happening because I'd ended up with one of the leads. All four of us couldn't have played that one character, so I had. Even though everybody had agreed and had signed off on the arrangement at the time, it was obvious now that egos had gotten bruised. Maybe they'd felt that I'd been placed out in front and they'd been my backup. I hadn't seen it that way at all.

One of the calls I got was from Chris Stokes. He has been around and heard a lot of stuff, but even he couldn't believe what he was hearing. Nobody else could either. Everybody was as shocked as I was. It was hard listening to that interview. I couldn't understand where all the negativity was coming from. The DJs didn't have to feed them, either. They just launched and kept on going. Their attitude, the tone of voice. It was all very, very negative.

A lot of people heard that interview. It even got repeated in its entirety several times over the next few days. Everybody who heard it was just as shocked as I was. They called and asked what was happening. My mom heard it, and she called too. She wanted to know what was going on, and I didn't have an answer for her. The tripped-out thing was that the public heard about it at the same time I heard about it. All of our problems hit the airwaves at the same time I found out about them. I don't get that. If there was some kind of a problem, why didn't we just talk it out? If you are friends with somebody, if you respect somebody, if you care about somebody, you owe it to them to come to them with the problem first. We had been through too much together for it to go down any other way. At least that's the way I see it. Whatever was going on wasn't as bad as they made it by going on the attack on the radio.

I think that it went down the way it did because of immaturity and the people that Fizz, Raz and Jarell had in their ears at the time. The immaturity came through in their not talking the problem out face-to-face, like men are supposed to do. I think that when the guys turned eighteen, they decided that they wanted to be their own men. They wanted to do things their way. All of that fits, and I can understand that. The older you get, the more you want to exercise some control over your career choices. But I felt it would always work in our best interests to rely on the experts to fill us in on what we didn't know. We became one of the largest music groups in the business by following the path and advice of people who knew what they were doing. But all of a sudden other folks seemed to have a lot of different ideas about how things should be handled. I'm just turning twenty now, and I don't consider myself a man yet. I'm getting there. I don't fool myself into thinking that I know everything. I'm learning something new every day. But one thing I do know, though, is that there's a right way to do something and a wrong way to do it. The way they chose was

∞ CRAZIEST B2K RUMOR ∞

There were a lot of them, but my favorite (or the worst) was that the four of us were making girls pregnant in cities across America by design. In other words, we wanted to have girls carrying our babies all across the country. PLEASE! GIVE ME A BREAK WITH THAT. Nothing could've been further from the truth. But like any good rumor, it had a life of its own.

wrong. Too many people got hurt, and that really wasn't necessary.

The three of them weren't being served well by their advisers. In fact, they were getting bad advice. I don't know if it was family, lawyers, agents or just some friends trying to get in on the game, but they were getting bad advice. Some of their issues may have been legit, but whoever advised them to go about it the way they did really screwed up, in my opinion. Somebody must've made them some big promises.

I talked to my manager, Chris, about it. At this time Chris was more like a mentor or a father figure to us than a manager. Though he was just as shocked and hurt as I was, he suggested that I keep cool and not make the situation any worse than it was by attacking them back. I understood that things happen and that most people feel that what they're doing at the time is right. I didn't hate anybody for what they did. But I will freely admit that I was hurt and pissed that it went down like it did.

What people don't know is that we even tried to fix the relationship. Even after the radio thing went down, we let the rumors cool down a little, and then we—me, Chris, Marques and everybody else they slammed—reached out to them.

We all hung out with J-Boog one night. On another night all of us went to dinner with Fizz. On both occasions I could tell that my friends were deeply conflicted by the sudden shift in events. They were about to make a big step, and I'm not sure

that they had thought it all through. Fizz and I started reminiscing about the good times on the road. And as I was sitting with Jarell, I actually forgot for a second why we were all there. It seemed so natural just hanging with him that I forgot that we were dealing with a crisis. It looked for a moment like things were going to get healed, but that feeling didn't last long. We heard them do another interview with a radio station in Chicago. The three of them were taking calls and dissin' everybody again. We had tried to be cool with them; what they were doing wasn't cool at all.

Chris and Marques were like my family now. They were there for me when I needed them. Fizz, J-Boog and Raz might have had some points that they were concerned with. Truthfully speaking, it was not about Chris or T.U.G.'s wrong doings. It was personal. And for me it was about loyalty. They went about things in a very negative way. And even though we were tight and we were boys, I couldn't go along with them making false statements. I couldn't have that. B2K breaking up was the very last thing in the world I wanted to have happen. But my bottom line was that I couldn't hang if they were going to go on dissing those that made us the supergroup we were. There was a lot of bad, ugly talk going on, and I wasn't hearing it.

Then on January 3, the final diss came through on the Internet. There was a picture of Fizz, Raz and J-Boog signing up with a new management company. That kind of made everything definite. B2K

I DON'T FOOL MYSELF INTO THINK-
ING THAT I KNOW EVERYTHING. I'M
LEARNING SOMETHING NEW EVERY
DAY. BUT ONE THING I DO KNOW,
THOUGH, IS THAT THERE'S A RIGHT
WAY TO DO SOMETHING AND A
WRONG WAY TO DO IT. THE WAY
THEY CHOSE WAS WRONG. TOO
MANY PEOPLE GOT HURT, AND THAT
REALLY WASN'T NECESSARY.

was over. Statements were released to the press. It was official. To set the record straight, I had my mom and attorney audit the Ultimate Group and found no mishandling nor theft of funds.

In one article, it was written up that the reason given for our breakup was that we had fallen victim to "inner turmoil." That's a good enough explanation—it covers our sudden rise to the top, the sudden fame, sudden prestige, the sudden wealth and the sudden fall. No matter how prepared you are, sudden stardom is not the easiest thing to handle. A lot of people can't: that public spotlight can get mighty hot. Our whole thing burned out just as suddenly as it had begun. Inner turmoil had taken its toll.

While going through all of this, I also became aware that I had first hooked up with the crew and we had become B2K in early January 2000. Now here it was early January 2004, and it was all over. I guess you could call that ironic. I didn't feel like laughing, but it was kind of funny in a way. We had jumped in, bonded, soared to the top and had a sudden crash landing all in three short years. Those were action-packed years, to be sure, but now that they were over, the time seemed short. I think I really enjoyed like ninety percent of the trip. The other ten percent? Well, stuff happens. You can't be happy all of the time—that's impossible, life doesn't work that way. Even the most successful and happy people in the world won't be happy one hundred percent of the time. Take somebody like Steven Spielberg, for example. I'm sure he has a wonderful and fantastic life. But I know that he isn't happy all of the time. Most of the time, yes. But not all. Ninety percent is pretty darn good for me or anybody else.

Now that I've had some time to think about things, I see them in a couple of different ways. For one thing, in our case a strong bond was everything, but in the end it wasn't enough. Once the individual plans became too unrealistic, once they weren't grounded in reality any longer, we started having problems. And once that negativity got in there, we had a whole other issue on our hands. Nothing should be done for spite. That ain't no motive. Things should always be handled, as much as possible, from a place of love and respect and the desire to really get things done. In the end, everything will come into the light.

In another sense the experience of the breakup taught me a lot about life. I learned that there will come a time when somebody really, really close to me, who I care about, will pass and go on to a different world. I'm kind of mentally prepared for that. That's what life is all about: It's a journey, and nothing stays the same.

When I was feeling kind of low about things, someone reminded me that the Beatles, possibly the greatest group in history, had broken up too. I'm sure that at one time they probably felt like it would go on forever. Just like us. Even the Temptations, the group that we wanted to grow old like, had gone through several breakups and personnel changes. That was some interesting history, but right now I was faced with the reality that I was suddenly a solo performer. That transition was going to be sick.

Chapter VIII

BETTER**DAYS**

MOVE THE CLOCK AHEAD FIVE YEARS.

THE FUTURE? The future is a mystery—but I'm in love with it. I'm seeing good things happening. I've had a wonderful run up until this point, and I don't intend to stop now. I intend to keep doing what I'm doing. I'm going to go with the flow of life and deal with whatever God puts before me.

I was hooked into the B2K matrix for so long that I find some habits are hard to break. When we weren't on the road, we'd call each other first thing in the morning to check on what was happening that day. On some mornings I catch myself reaching for the phone. I've got to be truthful—I miss the guys and I miss the adventure we shared together. I'm not exaggerating when I say that we had wonderful, fantastic times together—nothing will ever change that. We touched thousands of people with our music, and they touched our lives in return. Now there is a new adventure being written, and I'm looking forward to living it.

In the immediate future, I have my first solo album coming out in early 2005. A solo tour is being put together for the summer of 2005. That's going to be wild. My second movie, *Fat Albert,* should be arriving in the theaters around Christmas 2004. I'm playing a not-so-nice guy in this one—Reggie. Marques and myself are doing a film for Paramount Films entitled "Street Soldiers."

I was asked recently which I liked to do best: singing, dancing or acting. The truth is, I love all three. They are very different disciplines, but I want to master them all. I guess my desire is a result of having that entertainment gene in the bloodline. I want to be an all-around entertainer, and everything that I do points me toward that goal.

The singing and dancing come natural to me. I want to be the best at what I do, so I constantly rehearse. Once I get it down I keep going until I know a piece backwards and forwards. Even though dance—movement—provides room for improvisation, I want to know the routine cold before I allow myself to expand on it and improv something on the spot. I also have a vocal coach now who is helping me be an even better singer. For all I've been through, I am amazed sometimes at how much I still don't know about what I do best—singing and dancing.

Acting is a different ball game. From my very first time in front of the camera, I knew that this was

111

some serious business. I have so much respect for actors and those people who take the craft seriously. It's a challenge for me because I am still so new at it. I love the challenge. And I love the research involved in it too. I study the roles that Denzel Washington, Tom Cruise, Leonardo DiCaprio and Will Smith have played over the years. I check out the different ways they approach a particular character. There's a lot to be learned just watching these guys work. When those top guys get a good role, there's nothing like watching the masters working out. It might be kind of surprising, but I really like Martin Lawrence as an actor. He can go from funny to serious in a heartbeat. All things considered, film right now is really looking good for me, and I want to keep at it.

I appreciate the fact that I'm in a good position now. I feel that I can find out firsthand, from the people who are doing things, exactly what is happening. If I want to know about directing—when you should move the camera, how you compose a good shot—I can talk to some of the best directors in the business and learn from them. If I want to know about choreography, I have access to some of the finest creative minds around. All of that is good. It's like a win-win situation.

My musical taste is all over the place. I can pull up any kind of music that I want on my computer, and I do. The singers that I study are mostly gospel singers. Kim Burrell, Karen Clark Sheard, Dawkins and Dawkins—each artist is great in their own way, and I pick up a lot about performing just listening to them sing. They knock me out every time I listen to them.

Move the clock ahead five years. I will be twenty-five. Marriage and kids? Maybe. What I'm certain about is that I want to be doing more of what I'm doing now. Just more of it. More records. More live performances. More movies. More and better. Eventually I plan on getting into the production side of movies. That's the action that takes place behind the camera.

Beyond the entertainment, though, I would like to perhaps own a nice restaurant, invest in real estate and run some Pop Warner Little League teams for underprivileged youth. I see myself in the role of mentor. I feel that I can be a positive role model who can guide some talented kids in a good direction.

Even though I have been described a couple of times as a "heartthrob," that's not really me. I don't see myself that way. I'm not the guy that clubs all the time and hits the hot bling spots on the circuit. Don't get me wrong—I can party with the best of them. I can do that, but I'm more likely to spend quality time chilling with my family or a special lady. That doesn't sound like heartthrob behavior to me.

I think of myself as an extremely lucky guy who is enjoying his life. I am a very fortunate person to be doing what I'm doing. I feel that I was put on this earth to entertain, and that's what I will continue to do. If there is any one thing that I've learned in the past few years, it's that life is all about making mistakes and learning. I believe that if you go into any situation with a strong will, an open mind and a kind heart, God will bless you. He has certainly blessed me.

Like I've said before, I appreciate where I am now, and I've made a promise to myself not to waste time or energy on any bs. Life is too short and I'm having too good a time to blow it. Drugs? Bad relationships? Please—who's got the time for that kind of insanity?

It's all about making mistakes and learning. I'm learning.

And to all of the fans who supported me—I love them. They are responsible for putting me where I am today. They have stuck with me through good times and hard times. I appreciate them. I really care about them. I want them all to take the journey with me into the future. This is not a good-bye. This is just until the next time.

Peace.

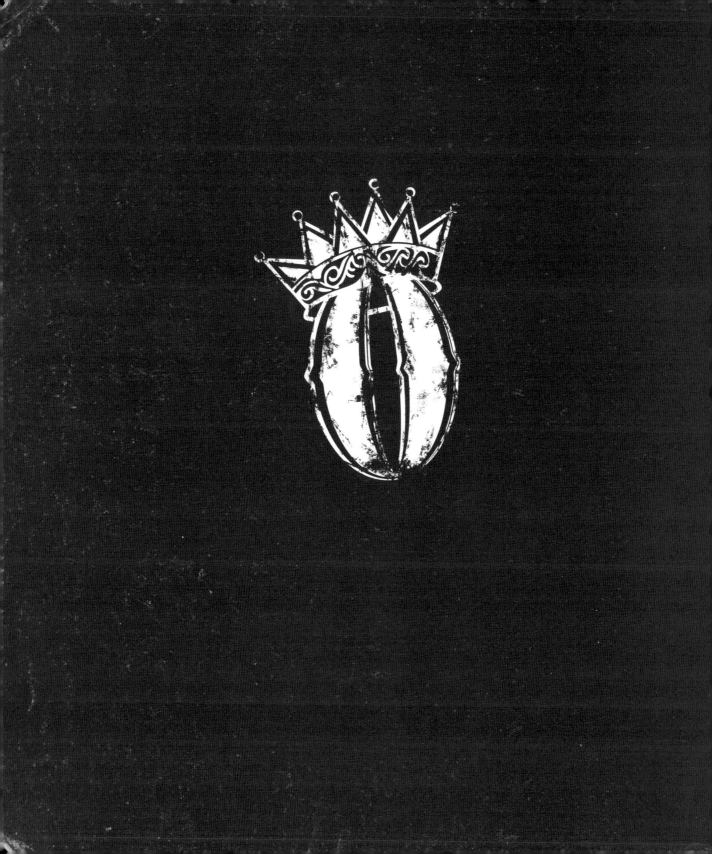